IMAGES
of America

BLUEFIELD IN
THE 1940s

IT'S ABOUT TIME. Snooks Charlton is shown glancing at his watch before taking off on another round to transport people of the city in a Tri-City Traction bus. Tri-City Traction operated the streetcar line that connected Bluefield and Princeton, West Virginia, with Bluefield, Virginia. The city replaced its streetcars with buses at the beginning of the 1940s and transformed many of its motormen to bus drivers. (Photograph by Mel Grubb.)

ON THE COVER: A color guard made up of representatives of the three branches of the military—the U.S. Marine Corps, U.S. Army, and U.S. Navy—led the city's huge "Heroes' Day Parade" on July 4, 1945. The parade honored S.Sgt. J. I. "Junior" Spurrier of Bluefield, who received the Congressional Medal of Honor during World War II, and also honored all service personnel as well as everyone who helped with the war effort. An estimated 25,000 to 30,000 people lined the city's streets to view the parade. (Photograph by Ellis Leon Martin.)

IMAGES
of America

BLUEFIELD IN THE 1940s

William R. "Bill" Archer

ARCADIA
PUBLISHING

Published by Arcadia Publishing
Charleston SC, Chicago IL, Portsmouth NH, San Francisco CA

Library of Congress Catalog Card Number: 2008933610

For all general information contact Arcadia Publishing at:
Telephone 843-853-2070
Fax 843-853-0044
E-mail sales@arcadiapublishing.com
For customer service and orders:
Toll-Free 1-888-313-2665

Visit us on the Internet at www.arcadiapublishing.com

The city of Bluefield is a remarkable place due primarily to its people. This book is dedicated to three of those people—my friends Heber Stafford, Mel Grubb, and the late Eva Vest Easley.

CONTENTS

ACKNOWLEDGMENTS

This marks the seventh book in Arcadia Publishing's Image of America series that I have been honored to write, and therefore, I would like to express my appreciation to the publisher for its commitment to preserving the images and stories that make the cities, towns, communities, counties, and states of this nation great.

First I would like to thank my wife, Evonda Archer, for her constant support, which makes this and all of our Arcadia projects possible. I would also like to thank Vera Hambrick, who inspired this book by sharing the photographs her father, Ellis Leon Martin, took of the July 4, 1945, Heroes' Day Parade in Bluefield. I thank Mel Grubb, who has created a photographic history of the city that is truly remarkable, and David McNeil, who now owns Grubb Photo Service. I also thank Heber Stafford, who never tires of demonstrating his love for his hometown. I thank my friend Dr. C. Stuart McGehee and the Eastern Regional Coal Archives of Bluefield's Craft Memorial Library for his help on this project and Edwin D. Seymour, nephew of the great artist Joseph Dodd, for tracking down photographs of his uncle.

As in all book projects, many people assisted by sharing images for the book. I thank all who shared images, including Joe Davidson, Charles Thompson, Art Riley, George Litz, Tom and Mary Jane Farmer, Susan Cooper Snyder, Dick Copeland, Joe and Janice Saunders, Elizabeth Gearheart, Ann B. Carlock, Cecil and Eleanor Smith, Ruth Surratt, Helen Stamoulis, Joe and Janice Sanders, Dr. J. I. Rodgin, Barbara Lewis, Don Neal, Frank Davis, Wanda Runion, John Nelson, Frank Bolden, the Graham Historical Society, Tom Colley and Randy Deason of the *Bluefield Daily Telegraph*, Carlton Viar, Jack White, Bill Blankenship, Tony Whitlow of the Those Who Served Museum, and the people of Bluefield.

INTRODUCTION

Bluefield emerged as a city because of a fluke of nature; it was the high point for east-and-west traffic on the Norfolk and Western (N&W) Railway from the Atlantic Ocean to the east and the Ohio River to the west. The "hump," as it was called, enabled trainmen to assemble eastbound trains of loaded coal cars by applying and releasing brakes and not requiring locomotive power. But the city eventually discovered its place in the world as a result of the efforts of enterprising people who called Bluefield home. The city grew from what was literally a cow pasture in 1882 into a city of 5,000 people when it was incorporated in 1889. But Bluefield didn't reach its full potential until the 1940s.

The great jazz pianist Teddy Weatherford, who grew up in Bluefield, gained international fame as a stride pianist in the 1940s, just as the city he called home during his formative years hit its stride during those years as well. Bluefield was a hub of regional activity that saw its birth in the post–New Deal industrialism ushered in by Franklin Delano Roosevelt and was propelled into the global spotlight as a result of World War II.

Bluefield residents became world citizens as a result of the war, cheering on Academy Award-winning actress Greer Garson, star of *Mrs. Minniver*, when she appeared in Bluefield to boost war bond sales on September 4, 1942. The patriotic nationalism that emerged during the war years appeared to explode on July 4, 1945, when a crowd of 25,000 to 30,000 people observed the Heroes' Day Parade in the city. That spirit of patriotic euphoria continued through the decade, as a (then) record one-day crowd of 13,363 people came to Bluefield on September 28, 1948, to see the touring railroad show of original documents including the Magna Carta, Declaration of Independence, U.S. Constitution, and other historical artifacts associated with the democratic experience that traveled aboard "the Freedom Train."

The U.S. Census Bureau indicates that Bluefield reached its peak population of 21,332 in 1950, and although the city was West Virginia's most racially diverse city, it was a divided city throughout the 1940s. Jim Crow segregation prevented much interaction between black and white Bluefielders, but that didn't stop progress in the city's African American community. Bluefield State College celebrated its 50th anniversary in 1945 with a faculty that included inspiring professors representing the nation's top universities. The city's black-owned business and professional community flourished, but equal access to all public services would have to wait for another decade.

The city played an important role in World War II through supplying many of her brave sons and daughters to fight in the war and by keeping the trains running through Bluefield to fuel the nation's incredible war machine. Less well known is the fact that National Electric Coil received the government contract to supply electric motors for the navy's PT boat program. Also, an enterprising lumberman, J. B. Belcher, found a way to cash in on the thousands of empty N&W Railway coal cars returning from the East Coast by asking the railroaders to haul back the fine teak wood and mahogany timber merchant sailors filled their supply ships with as ballast to replace the cargo they delivered to troops fighting in the Pacific theater of the war.

Despite all of the major developments taking shape in the 1940s, this is a story about people like postman Elijah Meadows, who knew everything about everything and delivered the mail twice a day when postage was 2¢; Ens. Ulvert "Fuzzy" Moore, who gave his life at the Battle of Midway in Torpedo Squadron 8's Light Brigade–style attack that turned the tide of the war in the Pacific; Dr. William A. Brown, who operated St. Mary's Hospital in Bluefield to serve the city's African American community; Eulalia "Feet" Magann, who served as a WAVE during World War II and came back home to teach hundreds of Bluefield youngsters how to swim; and Dr. John Forbes Nash Jr., who dreamed of becoming a great mathematician and eventually received the Nobel Prize in Economics for his labors.

Thus Bluefield's story in the 1940s is a story of how people dreamed great dreams and accomplished great things. It's not a perfect story, but it is a story filled with fascinating details at every turn in the path.

One

THE CROSSROADS OF
ENERGY AND POWER

TAPE MEASURE. Bluefield fire chief Ernest L. McClure is shown reading the punch tape from the city's pull box station system, a system the department acquired from the city of Cincinnati, Ohio, when that city outgrew it. The system featured several pull box stations strategically placed throughout the city and linked by electrical wires. Each station sent a unique electrical impulse to the central station that was imprinted on a paper tape and triggered a series of bell rings that indicated the location of the call to the firemen. Chief McClure and his wife, Virginia, lived at 517 North Street in Bluefield. (Photograph by Mel Grubb.)

LIGHT WORK. Bluefield fire chief Ernest L. McClure demonstrates operations of the new lights on one of the city's fire trucks. The city's fire department was headquartered on the city's north side in the 1940s at 101–105 Roanoke Street. (Photograph by Mel Grubb.)

WITH A SONG IN MY HEART. The city of Bluefield was noted for the beautiful music made by her residents. Marion Smith is shown here accompanying herself on piano at her home at 120 Summers Street. Smith was a well-known area performer, but she also performed as far away as New York City. Still, like many performers, she maintained a day job as well and worked as a clerk at the Bluefield Jewelry Company at 526 Princeton Avenue. (Photograph by Mel Grubb.)

A CITY OF DESTINY. This aerial photograph of Bluefield around 1940 shows the city near its peak. The old Norfolk and Western roundhouse, shown in the left center portion of the photograph, provided jobs for about 500 railroaders, and the downtown's dominant West Virginian Hotel with its 12 stories was the largest man-made structure in the state south of Charleston, West Virginia. It is easy to date the photograph well before 1947, because the site preparation work had not yet begun on the city's municipally owned Scott Street Parking Garage. (Courtesy of *Bluefield Daily Telegraph* archives.)

TWO TO CROON. Frank Sinatra (right) and trumpet great Ziggy Elman posed for this publicity photograph by J. Vincent Lewis of Nunnaly's Studio at 408 Raleigh Street prior to a concert by the Tommy Dorsey Orchestra on May 8, 1941. The concert was held at Jack Craft's Consolidated Bus Terminal at 2100 Princeton Avenue. (Courtesy of *Bluefield Daily Telegraph* archives.)

11

ALL THAT AT THE MICK OR MACK. Morris Harris (in apron at left) and an unidentified store clerk are shown standing at the entrance to the Mick or Mack (groceries and meats) store at 613 Bland Street. The store was owned by B. E. Tabor and had stiff competition from scores of grocery stores in the area, most of which were locally owned, but some, like the Kroger store across the street at 640 Bland, were in the infancy of supermarkets. Kroger operated three stores in Bluefield in the 1940s. (Courtesy of Tom and Mary Jane Farmer.)

END OF THE STREETCAR LINE. The start of the 1940s marked the end of Bluefield's popular Tri-City Traction streetcar line that connected the Norfolk and Western passenger station on Princeton Avenue with Bluefield, Virginia, and Princeton, West Virginia, the tri-cities of the business name. One streetcar is shown here on College Avenue. (From the author's collection.)

WEST END ANCHOR. The old West Virginia Armature Company building shown here was one of Bluefield's earliest electrical motor manufacturing and repair facilities. Although this picture is from the 1930s, the collection of buildings in the background represents Bluefield State College (BSC) prior to the construction of Conley Hall or most of the other buildings that form the BSC campus's distinctive appearance. BSC celebrated its 50th anniversary in 1945. West Virginia Armature was located at 2 Pine Street and was flanked by the Norfolk and Western Railway to the north. (Courtesy of Frank Davis.)

THE AVENUE. Other businesses in addition to West Virginia Armature, National Electric Coil, Feuchtenberger Bakery, Wade School, and the Coca-Cola Bottling Plant combined to make Bluefield Avenue a hub of activity in the city in the 1930s and 1940s. (From the author's collection.)

MAN WITH A PLAN. Famed Bluefield architect Alex B. Mahood (left, with vest buttoned) is shown working with a young architect as they examine documents in Mahood's studio in the penthouse of the Law and Commerce Building. Mahood had a hand in the design of almost every public structure in Bluefield as well as several of the stately private residences in the city. (Courtesy of the Eastern Regional Coal Archives.)

A STITCH IN TIME. Charles V. Rondinelli makes a man's suit jacket at his tailor shop in Room 203 of the Bluefield Coal and Coke Building on Federal Street in Bluefield. Rondinelli was well known for his excellence in tailoring. (Photograph by Mel Grubb.)

THE BUSINESS OF SAVING SOLES. Jimmy Maiola is shown repairing a shoe in his shoe repair shop at 618 Federal Street in Bluefield, across the street from the Elizabeth Kee Federal Building. Maiola was a native of Italy who returned home frequently to visit family and friends. He passed away in his homeland on his last visit. His Bluefield residence was 406 Rogers Street. (Photograph by Mel Grubb.)

Classical Violin. Vincent Paoliello was the leader of the popular Paoliello String Quartet, which was in great demand for local and regional performances, according to Dr. J. I. Rodgin. Rodgin's mother, Anna Groman Rodgin, was a member of the ensemble. Paoliello was president of Mann Piano Company at 605 Bland Street. Bluefield banker James E. Mann was vice president of the company, and George E. Mann Jr. was secretary/treasurer. Paoliello lived at 308 Tazewell Avenue. (Photograph by Mel Grubb.)

TURN YOUR RADIO ON. A very young Roy Acuff is shown here second from the right with a group of unidentified local musicians who gathered at the WHIS-AM Radio studios at 621 Commerce Street, likely to do some promotional work for one of Acuff's new records or to promote a local concert. WHIS—named for Hugh Ike Shott, owner of the station and editor/publisher of the *Bluefield Daily Telegraph*—went on the air on June 27, 1929. The studio was first located in the West Virginian Hotel but moved to Commerce Street in 1935 and into the studio seen here, where it became affiliated with the National Broadcasting Corporation's Blue Network, in 1939. (Courtesy of Ruth Surratt.)

WEATHER OR NOT. Louis Zaltzman, a Norfolk and Western Railway timekeeper, is shown at the railroad's Pocahontas Division headquarters on Summers Street at Raleigh Street checking the high and low temperatures at the railroad's weather station. In 1939, Bluefield's tireless supporter, H. Edward "Eddie" Steele, came up with the idea to promote Bluefield's mild summers by touting Bluefield as "Nature's Air-conditioned City" and distributing free lemonade any time the temperature in the city reached 90 degrees Fahrenheit. Steele was secretary of the Greater Bluefield Chamber of Commerce at the time, and Zaltzman was the closest thing the city had to an official weatherman, so Steele enlisted his help with the unique and lasting weather-related promotion. Louis and his wife, Freda A., lived at 320 Stowers Street. (Photograph by Mel Grubb.)

CHECK AND BALANCE. An unidentified meter reader is shown here outside the Norfolk and Western Railway Pocahontas Division headquarters taking a water reading. Stone masons from Italy built most of the city's distinctive retaining walls, like the wall shown behind the water company worker here. (Photograph by Mel Grubb.)

FOR THE LOVE OF THE LEMON. Greater Bluefield Chamber of Commerce president Will Cole (far left) receives the first glass of lemonade served by a "Lemonade Lassie" in the summer of 1941, the first time the temperature in Bluefield hit the 90-degree mark after the chamber decided to adopt the promotion. The program was suspended during World War II because of sugar rationing, but from 1941 through the summer of 2008, the chamber has made good on its promise on 197 days. In many years, there were no 90- or 90-plus-degree days, including 2008. The record years to date are 1988, when the chamber served lemonade 17 times, and 2007, when the chamber served lemonade 18 times. (Courtesy of the Eastern Regional Coal Archives.)

YOU CAN GET ANYTHING YOU WANT. Popular Bluefield restaurateur Jimmy Rantis operated Jimmy's Restaurant at 636 Princeton Avenue through Bluefield's heydays, featuring a large fish tank in the front and offering fresh seafood brought in daily from Virginia Beach, Virginia. Rantis was a tireless community servant and proud representative of the city's thriving Greek community. (Courtesy of Helen Stamoulis.)

DEDICATED HEALER. Dr. William A. Brown owned and operated St. Mary's Hospital on Bland Street in Bluefield. The hospital was devoted to the care and treatment of the city's African American families. Brown was born on a former plantation in Wytheville, Virginia, and graduated from the Leonard School of Medicine and Pharmacy of Shaw University in Raleigh, North Carolina. (Courtesy of Frank Bolden, Esq.)

20

THE TONG SONG. William A. Atwell, manager of American Service Company, the city's ice manufacturing facility at 111 Poplar Street, is shown using tongs to move a 100-pound block of ice. The American Service Company provided ice for home iceboxes but also had a contract to supply ice in large 300-pound blocks for use in the Norfolk and Western Railway's refrigeration cars, which kept food fresh on long rail trips. The railroad had to replenish its store of ice every 100 miles, especially in the hot summer months. Even in Nature's Air-conditioned City, Atwell had a cool job. He and his wife, Lorraine, lived at 2200 Wythe Avenue. (Photograph by Mel Grubb.)

ICE IS NICE. William A. Atwell moves a block of ice by hand. Bluefield Ice and Cold Storage Company, American Service Company's parent company, also distributed National Premium and Bohemian Beer, Fort Pitt Beer and Ale, Barbarossa, and Red Top Beer and Ale. (Photograph by Mel Grubb.)

THE PRIDE OF BLUEFIELD. The Riley-Vest Post No. 9 of the American Legion sponsored one of the premier junior drum and bugle corps in the nation, earning national titles in 1936 and 1939, the same year that Helen "Sis" Warden, daughter of corps founder David Warden, earned the title of National American Legion Majorette Queen. David Warden's unexpected death in 1942 and the fact that most of the male members of the group entered the military after the Japanese attack on Pearl Harbor on December 7, 1941, spelled the end of the unit's parade days. The group reorganized for the Heroes' Day Parade on July 4, 1945, and held its last major reunion in 1971. (Courtesy of Grubb Photo Service.)

PLAY BALL. The last prewar Bluefield Blue-Gray baseball team is shown here posing for a team picture in 1941 at the team's new ballpark, Bowen Field. Although there were several coalfield teams through the years, there was only one Coalfield League, a Class D league that existed from 1937 through the 1941 season and included the Beckley, West Virginia, Bengals; the Huntington, West Virginia, Booster Bees; the Logan, West Virginia, Indians; the Williamson, West Virginia, Colts; the Welch, West Virginia, Miners; and the Bluefield Blue-Grays. League teams played a 120-game schedule, and the most famous alumnus of the league was Stan "The Man" Musial, who spent his first two years as a professional baseball player, 1938 and 1939, with the Williamson Colts. (Courtesy of Grubb Photo Service.)

NOBEL LAUREATE IN TRAINING. Dr. John Forbes Nash Jr. (back row, standing fourth from the right) is shown with a group of young Bluefielders gathered at the home of Dr. J. E. and Mabel H. Blaydes before traveling to the Bluefield Country Club for the annual Junior Cotillion Club Dance in 1940. Although not in order, the young people shown here include: Nancy Blaydes, Betty Clair Frazier, Sally Anne Mundy, Nancy O'Keeffe, Barbara Shunk, Anne St. Clair, Mary Lou St. Clair, Jean Smith, Mary Jo Wagner, Jane Wagner, Betty Wellford, Jean Williams, Dot Wilson, Charlotte Woods, Conrad Brevick, Conrad Crowe, Albert Kemper, Ken Greiser, Guy Lawhead, Jim Moore, Johnny Nash, Hughitt Mattox, Billy Owen, Brookie Taylor, George Walker, Sam Jackson, Tom Jackson, Billy Greenspon, Bill Thomas, Bob Scott, and Joe Sanders. (Courtesy of Joe and Janice Sanders.)

Two

BLUEFIELD GOES TO WAR

READ ALL ABOUT IT. A group of 100 newsboys took to the streets on December 7, 1941, with an extra edition of the *Sunset News* carrying the news about the Japanese attack on the U.S. Pacific Fleet stationed at Pearl Harbor in the Hawaiian Islands. The *Sunset News* was Bluefield's afternoon newspaper, while the flagship, *Bluefield Daily Telegraph*, continues to serve residents as the morning newspaper. There have only been five extra editions in the history of the two newspapers—announcing the armistice ending World War I, this edition, the German and Japanese surrenders, and the terrorist attacks on the United States on September 11, 2001. (Courtesy of *Bluefield Daily Telegraph* archives.)

A NATION'S INDUSTRIAL MIGHT EMERGES. Willis E. Cowling Sr. is shown here fabricating a gear for a piece of Norfolk and Western Railway equipment at the railroad's shops in the Bluefield yard. Like many American cities, Bluefield was believed to have been targeted by Hitler's war machine during World War II because of its strategic importance in the coal industry. As the war intensified, the city conducted air raid drills under the watchful eyes of the local American Red Cross. Cowling and his wife, Lucille, lived at 904 1/2 Raleigh Terrace. (Photograph by Mel Grubb.)

RECAPPING THE NEWS. With the scarcity of rubber during World War II, recapping tires, like the worker at Reid and Boice Tire and Tread Company is shown doing here, was the only way to keep moving in the war years. Reid and Boice, owned by Otis E. Reid and Lemdall Boice, was at 610 Raleigh Street. (Photograph by Mel Grubb.)

BROTHERS IN ARMS. Twin brothers Marvin (left) and Melvin "Mel" Grubb, the sons of Everett and Ella Grubb of 1008 Lyndale Avenue, entered the military together a few weeks after they graduated from Beaver High School in May 1943. While Marvin went to work with Appalachian Power Company after the war, Melvin returned home to pursue a dream of being a professional photographer. Most of the images in this book, as well as most of the images that define the history of Bluefield, exist because of Melvin L. Grubb's passion for photography. (Courtesy of David McNeil.)

THE POWER BEHIND THE WAR. Tom Kitts, an armature winder with Bluefield's National Electric Coil Company, examines the wires of an industrial-sized armature. Prior to the start of the war, Charles Edison (the son of Thomas A. Edison), who served as Secretary of the Navy in Pres. Franklin D. Roosevelt's administration, became friends with National Electric Coil's leadership, J. W. "Red" Overstreet and brothers John and Charlie Cruise. Edison sent wartime contracts to National Coil, including a contract to supply the electric motors for the U.S. Navy's PT boat program. National would later supply some of the component parts of the Relativistic Heavy Ion Collider at the Brookhaven Lab in New York, which creates radioactive materials for medical use. Kitts and his wife, Virginia, lived at 907 Rockbridge Street. (Photograph by Mel Grubb.)

POWERFUL STATEMENT. The young men shown here in 1944 were students of the Bluefield Mercer County Vocational School Mining School. The students were in training to become part of an underground army of coal miners that supplied the coal to forge the steel of the nation's war machine. Coal miners received a draft deferment because their work was considered essential to the war effort. (Courtesy of the Eastern Regional Coal Archives.)

TOTAL EFFORT. World War II had an impact on people of all ages, with all Americans contributing to the war effort. This photograph shows a carpenter who appears to be making slots for a mobile mail distribution vehicle. Postal workers sorted mail in both buses and railroad cars. (Photograph by Mel Grubb.)

THE BEST AND BRIGHTEST. Ulvert M. "Fuzzy" Moore was born in Williamson, West Virginia, but came to Bluefield when his father, L. E. Moore, became director of the Norfolk and Western Railway YMCA in Bluefield. Fuzzy graduated from Beaver High School in 1935, Bluefield College in 1937, and West Virginia University in 1939, and he entered his nation's service through the U.S. Naval Reserve and became a U.S. Navy flier. (Courtesy of Heber Stafford.)

FLIGHT INTO HISTORY. Ens. Ulvert Mathew Moore was assigned to the USS *Hornet* aircraft carrier and was one of the fliers of Torpedo Squadron 8 who sacrificed their lives during the June 4, 1942, Battle of Midway, which turned the tide of the war in the Pacific during World War II. Ensign Moore, who was re-nicknamed "Whitey" by his comrades because of his light-colored hair, is profiled along with the other fliers in Torpedo Squadron 8 in Robert Mrazek's book *A Dawn Like Thunder*. (Courtesy of *Bluefield Daily Telegraph* archives.)

BAND OF BROTHERS. Members of the Bluefield-based 150th Infantry Division regimental band are shown here at Camp Shelby, Mississippi. Col. William E. Eubank commanded the 1,500 officers and men of the 150th, who were on active duty at the start of World War II and were sent to protect the Panama Canal. From left to right are (first row) J. H. Bone, Pfc. T. A. Yonce, G. Brandon, J. Vaughan, L. Henley, H. Hicks, C. Thompson, E. Miller, Cpl. J. Seagle, E. Taylor, W. Chicagus, and H. Eberhardt; (second row) T.Sgt. E. L. Stewart, S.Sgt. W. E. Hager, Sgt. O. H. Thorn, Pfc. T. W. Osborne, J. Perona, Cpl. A. S. Kovach, N. Howenstein, Pfc. R. B. Lee, S. Connelley, R. Kemper, Pfc. D. Steiner, J. Vitale, V. Rhode, Pfc. J. J. Becktel, and Sgt. J. E. Calloway; (third row) Pfc. W. H. French, R. Wolfe, Pfc. P. R. Small, Pfc. H. M. Chafin, Sgt. M. W. Steiner, Pfc. J. W. Lilly, G. McNally, A. Miller, Pfc. F. T. Lawson, Pfc. E. E. Charlton, E. Gabett, Pfc. W. F. Farris, and D. Chambers; (fourth row) Pfc. M. S. Grim Jr., Pfc. T. Horton, Pfc. R. Beckulhimer, Pfc. W. V. Weaver, Pfc. J. J. Harrison, Pfc. R. C. Henley, Pfc. J. R. Vermilyea, Pfc. D. T. Barton, Cpl. J. R. Meadows, and Sgt. G. W. Brown. (Courtesy of Heber Stafford.)

THE ART OF WAR. Pfc. Joseph Eldridge Dodd was coming into his own as an artist in 1942 when he was drafted into the U.S. Army and sent to the Pacific theater of the war, where he contracted a disease and was discharged early in 1945. He died on November 30, 1945, at age 38. Dodd, a Wood County, West Virginia, native, taught art at Bluefield State College and is considered to be one of the state's best artists. (Courtesy of Edwin D. Seymour.)

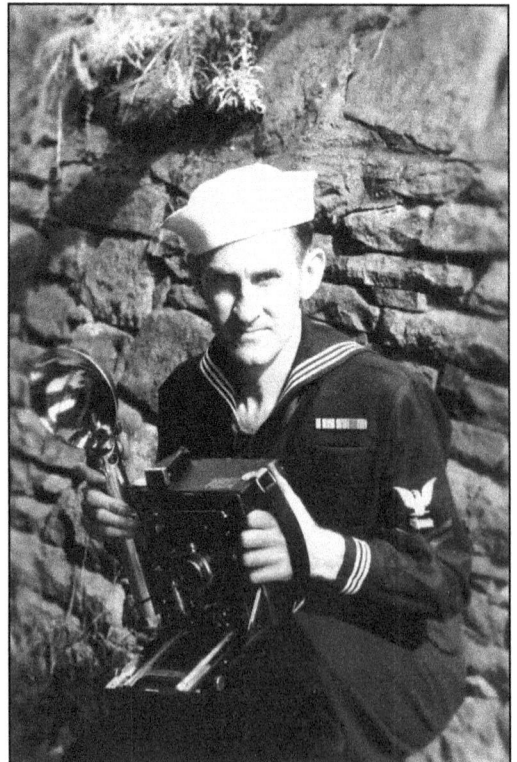

DEDICATED TO SERVICE. Sn. Ellis Leon Martin of the U.S. Navy was born in Maybeury, West Virginia, in 1909 but was raised in Bluefield after his mother died when he was young. He was a photographer in the navy but worked for the Norfolk and Western Railway after the war. Seaman Martin took all of the Heroes' Day Parade photographs included in this book. (Courtesy of Vera Hambrick.)

AIR SUPREMACY. Capt. William O. Bivens Jr. (standing, far right) commanded a B-24 Liberator as pilot at age 20. Bivens is shown with his crew. He only gave the museum the last names and the jobs of the men in his B-24 crew. From left to right are (first row) McKinnie (radio), Knaack (gunner), Finch (engineer), Martinsen (gunner), Takolo (gunner), and Pigg (gunner); (second row) Lourey (navigator), Peterson (bombardier), Holcomb (copilot), and Captain Bivens. After earning his law degree, Bivens served as Bluefield city solicitor for many years and was elected to the bench as a Mercer County Circuit Court judge. (Courtesy of the Those Who Served Museum.)

I SAW YOU LAST NIGHT AND GOT THAT OLD FEELING. This man, known by the name "Mister Arney" by photographer Mel Grubb, is shown servicing the huge band saw at Belcher Sawmill in Bluefield's East End. J. B. Belcher operated a successful lumber business and found an interesting way to improve his business during the war. Supply ships that carried troops, arms, and other cargo to the Pacific theater of the war used fine hardwood mahogany and teak logs to serve as ballast for their return to the port in Norfolk, Virginia. Belcher worked with Norfolk and Western locomotive engineers to bring the discarded logs back to Bluefield, where he transformed them into boards used in the regional furniture business. (Photograph by Mel Grubb.)

JUST THE TICKET. Charles G. "Henry" Farmer, an officer with the Bluefield City Police Department, puts a parking ticket on the windshield of an automobile illegally parked in Bluefield. Officer Farmer and his wife, Clara, lived at 1033 James Street. He was a beat officer in the downtown area and was best known for catching a man who robbed the First National Bank and tried to make a getaway on foot but took a wrong turn and was nabbed in a blind alley between the bank and the Shrine Club building on Federal Street. (Photograph by Mel Grubb.)

SERIOUS ABOUT PARKING. Officer G. "Henry" Farmer checks a city parking meter. With a scarcity of level ground in the city and a concentration of big buildings, on-street parking has been a challenge for the city for many years. (Photograph by Mel Grubb.)

GREER IS HERE. Hollywood movie star Greer Garson is shown entering Bluefield during a parade on Federal Street that took place at 11:30 a.m. on September 4, 1942. (Courtesy of Wanda Runion.)

ENCHANTED. Greer Garson waves to her fans during the parade in her honor from the Norfolk and Western passenger station up Federal Street to the West Virginian Hotel. A photographer with the *Sunset News* caught Garson as she waved to the crowd. (Courtesy of *Bluefield Daily Telegraph* archives.)

ELECTRIFYING REDHEAD. Greer Garson is shown in this photograph from the collection of Alex B. Mahood greeting her fans during her September 4, 1942, appearance in Bluefield as part of her war bond tour. The West Virginian Hotel was decked out in patriotic splendor for the event. "I love all of America. I love her freedom and I love her justice," Garson said from the West Virginian Hotel balcony. (Courtesy of the Eastern Regional Coal Archives.)

DRAWING A CROWD. People jammed Commerce Street in Bluefield just to get a glimpse of Greer Garson as she spoke from the West Virginian Hotel balcony, as shown in this photograph from Alex B. Mahood's collection. The Beaver High School band (in dark uniforms) is shown in the center foreground, and the famous American Legion Junior Drum and Bugle Corps is shown in the center of the picture in white uniforms. Local retail store owners closed up shop so everyone in town could participate in the event. (Courtesy of the Eastern Regional Coal Archives.)

A STAR FROM AFAR. English-born actress Greer Garson received an Academy Award in 1942 as best actress for her work in *Mrs. Minniver* and worked with the U.S. Treasury Department on a major tour promoting the sale of war bonds. She is shown here appearing on the second-floor balcony of the hotel. This photograph was taken from the sixth floor of the Law and Commerce Building. (Courtesy of Wanda Runion.)

SHOWING AT THE STATE. Glen Brewer loads a film into the projector of Bluefield's State Theater at 513 Commerce Street across from the balcony of the West Virginian Hotel. The theater opened a short time before Greer Garson's arrival and decorated its ticket window with sand bags and a mock machine gun to resemble a military position in honor of Garson's arrival. The State had a special showing of *Mrs. Minniver* in honor of the star's personal appearance. Glen and his wife, Geneva Brewer, lived at 1912 Princeton Avenue. The State was the city's newest motion picture theater in the 1940s and competed with the more established Colonial Theater at 610 Princeton Avenue, the Field Theater at 626 Princeton Avenue, and the Granada Theater at 537 Commerce Street. (Photograph by Mel Grubb.)

DEFENDERS. Heber Stafford is shown in 1944 while serving with the 28th Fighter Squadron, which protected the Panama Canal. In one of war's ironies, Heber's brother, A. F. "Red" Stafford, was also stationed in Panama with the 150th Infantry based in Bluefield. (Courtesy of Heber Stafford.)

LIFETIME OF SERVICE. Eulalia "Feet" (Francisco) Magann is shown in 1943 during her service as a specialist second class in the U.S. Navy WAVES (Women Accepted Volunteer Emergency Service). After the war, Magann, the wife of Mercer County Schools principal John W. Magann, taught generations of Bluefielders how to swim as a Red Cross volunteer swimming instructor. (Courtesy of the Those Who Served Museum.)

40

CIVIC ICON. Wallace W. "Squire" McNeal, a Spanish-American War veteran who served the city for many years as justice of the peace, died on August 30, 1944. Squire McNeal inspired the popular Louis Jordan song "Salt Pork, West Virginia." (Courtesy of *Bluefield Daily Telegraph* archives.)

COOPER'S NAVY. Radioman 2nd Class William Y. "Billy" Cooper is shown here soon after he entered the U.S. Navy during World War II. Billy and his bride, Emaline Cooper, built a home at 1013 Longview Avenue after the war. (Courtesy of Susan Cooper Snyder.)

THE WAR IN PICTURES. Joseph Schleifstein, a native of Sandomierz, poses with American soldiers and his German army captors following the liberation of the Buckenwald death camp by Allied forces in early April 1945. Capt. Max Kammer of Bluefield got a camera from a site where German soldiers were surrendering their weapons and took the photograph on April 12, 1945. Max Kammer's family was Lithuanian Jews who migrated to West Virginia in the late 1800s. His father, Harry Kammer, founded Kammer Furniture, a company that continues to serve Bluefield and the surrounding communities. Schleifstein was born on March 7, 1941, and arrived in Buckenwald on January 20, 1945. He now lives in New York City. Some of Captain Kammer's photographs are on display at the National Holocaust Museum in Washington, D.C. (Photograph by Max Kammer.)

Three

A SALUTE TO HEROES

ONE DOWN, ONE TO GO. The Bluefield Business and Professional Club decorated an old car to celebrate VE (Victory in Europe) Day (May 8, 1945) and in anticipation of VJ (Victory in Japan) Day (August 14, 1945) and drove it in the July 4, 1945, Heroes' Day Parade through the city. The club raised thousands of dollars to help finance the parade. (Courtesy of Vera Hambrick.)

BLUE RIBBON PANEL. Dignitaries from the military and federal, state, and local government stood at the platform at Mitchell Stadium for the Heroes' Day Parade salute with members of the Ashford General Hospital Band from White Sulphur Springs, seated on the back of the speakers' platform. Standing from left to right are Col. David R. Stinson, Lt. Col. Orin Jones, Col. Harry S. Bishop, the Reverend O'Ferrall Thompson, Lt. Col. Frank A. Hunter, U.S. Representative John Kee (D., WV), S.Sgt. J. I. "Junior" Spurrier, Henry Fortune, and U.S. Senator Chapman Revercomb (R., WV). (Courtesy of Vera Hambrick.)

HUMBLE HERO. S.Sgt. J. I. "Junior" Spurrier is shown after arriving in Mitchell Stadium following the Heroes' Day Parade through Bluefield. Spurrier fought in both the Pacific and European theaters of World War II and received the Congressional Medal of Honor, the Distinguished Service Cross, the French Croix de Guerre, and the Purple Heart with cluster for his service. Note the members of the Ashford General Hospital Band in the background. The posh Greenbrier Hotel was transformed into a military hospital during World War II. (Courtesy of Vera Hambrick.)

A NORMAL DAY IN BLUEFIELD. Sn. Ellis Leon Martin was home on leave from the U.S. Navy on July 4, 1945, and decided to take some pictures of the big parade in Bluefield. The All-Community Committee raised money for the event, which started promptly at 1:30 p.m. Seaman Martin took this photograph looking up Federal Street into the heart of Bluefield's downtown. Evans Flag and Decorating Company of Terre Haute, Indiana, was in charge of decorations. (Courtesy of Vera Hambrick.)

MAN OF THE HOUR. Although he didn't talk much about his time in the war, S.Sgt. J. I. "Junior" Spurrier stands to greet the crowd of 25,000 to 30,000 who attended the parade. Max Matz, chairman of the All-Community Committee, is seated in the back seat of Spurrier's car, and the driver is unidentified. (Courtesy of Vera Hambrick.)

STADIUM SET. S.Sgt. J. I. "Junior" Spurrier (in uniform above) and the other dignitaries who participated in the Heroes' Day Parade are shown arriving at Mitchell Stadium. The parade started at 1:30 p.m., and the program at the football field was set to start at 3:00 p.m. (Courtesy of Vera Hambrick.)

ANTICIPATION. Bluefield has a long tradition of hosting some incredible parades, like the July 4, 1945, Heroes' Day Parade Ellis Leon Martin photographed. After graduating from Beaver High School in Bluefield, Martin returned to McDowell County and opened his own photography studio. He returned to Iaeger, West Virginia, after the war but accepted a position with the Norfolk and Western Railway in 1947. Martin and his wife, Cathryn, had two daughters, Vera Hambrick and Martha Martin. He became active in the Boy Scouts of America and eventually was appointed a commissioner in the Boy Scouts. (Courtesy of Vera Hambrick.)

THROUGH TRAFFIC. A city police officer is shown in the intersection of Princeton Avenue and Federal Street keeping the flow of traffic moving as the crowd starts to build for the parade. (Courtesy of Vera Hambrick.)

HERE TO SERVE. In addition to moving coal through the region, Bluefield was also a hub of activity for transporting troops to and from the war on two fronts. The Bluefield Railroad Canteen, located in the Bluefield Norfolk and Western Railway passenger station, provided doughnuts and coffee for all the soldiers passing through the city and remained open 24 hours a day, every day of the week. (Courtesy of Vera Hambrick.)

CHRISTIAN SOLDIERS. The Salvation Army has had a presence in Bluefield since the early decades of the city, providing comfort to families at a time of great need during World War II. Note the group of young people on bicycles following the Salvation Army's patriotic display. (Courtesy of Vera Hambrick.)

IT'S BEEN A LONG, LONG TIME. A crowd of mostly women waits for the Heroes' Day Parade to pass while standing in front of the Lerner Shops, a women's apparel shop located at 416 Princeton Avenue. The faces show the anticipation for the end of the war and the return of husbands, fathers, and boyfriends. (Courtesy of Vera Hambrick.)

WHILE MEN TALK OF WAR. Ellis Leon Martin took this photograph of a conversation between four men, two older and two younger, in advance of the start of the parade. By July 4, 1945, all Americans were anxious to see an end to the global conflict that changed the nation. (Courtesy of Vera Hambrick.)

LAST HURRAH. The ranks of the nationally famous Bluefield Junior Drum and Bugle Corps had been decimated by 1945, with most able-bodied young men from the corps serving in the military somewhere. Two of the corps' founding members, Steve Riley and Harry Vest Jr., were killed in action in World War II, and Bluefield's American Legion post, Riley-Vest Post No. 9, remembers their sacrifice in its name. The group won a state title in 1947, but the days of national prominence were gone. Note the female color guard leading the parade compared to the male color guard during the prewar years shown on page 22. (Courtesy of Vera Hambrick.)

YOUNG RECRUITS. Membership with the Bluefield Junior Drum and Bugle Corps was a source of great pride for the group's members and to the families of those who belonged to the well-known organization. (Courtesy of Vera Hambrick.)

THE STREETS WERE PACKED. From his vantage point on the stone wall on the railroad side of Princeton Avenue, Ellis Leon Martin could see the crowds building with excitement on both sides of Federal Street. (Courtesy of Vera Hambrick.)

ROUGH RIDERS. A contingency of veterans of the Spanish-American War, fought in 1898, is shown prior to entering the line of march for the Heroes' Day Parade. The Spanish War veterans, who were directed by Isiah N. Hodges, followed the navy float and marched in front of the Beni-Kedem Shrine Drill Team. (Courtesy of Vera Hambrick.)

BEVY OF BEAUTIES. Several young ladies from the area wearing bathing suits rode on the American Legion float in the Heroes' Day Parade. The ladies represented posts in Bluefield and Princeton, West Virginia, and Pocahontas, Virginia. (Courtesy of Vera Hambrick.)

RED CROSS SERVES. Representatives of several services within the American Red Cross participated in the Heroes' Day Parade, including the Home Service Corps, the Junior Red Cross, Production, Administration, the Grey Ladies, Nurses Aides, Home Nursing, and the regular Red Cross automobile that was used in various drills, including blackout drills in the city. The local Red Cross personnel served at the Ashford General Hospital in White Sulphur Springs. (Courtesy of Vera Hambrick.)

HERE AND THERE. Ellis Leon Martin photographed the Red Cross Volunteer Services personnel as they passed his position on Princeton Avenue at Federal Street and continued on down Princeton Avenue in the direction of the Norfolk and Western Railway Pocahontas Division offices. (Courtesy of Vera Hambrick.)

HORSING AROUND. Bluefield businessman Marion B. "Post" Postlethwaite, who owned and operated an apartment building at 212 Ramsey Street in the city, is shown riding his horse through the intersection of Princeton Avenue and Federal Street. He was the subject of a couple of stories related to the parade. First, a young man saw him twirling his gold-headed cane prior to the start of the parade and asked: "Say mister. Are you a state senator?" Later, during the parade, his horse apparently got tired and sat down to rest in the middle of the parade, blocking progress until Postlethwaite could get him moving again. (Courtesy of Vera Hambrick.)

LOOKING INTO THE EAST END. Ellis Leon Martin photographed a part of Princeton Avenue to the east of Federal Street. Note the big clock in front of Henry Rodgin's jewelry store and the Matz Hotel, the tallest building on the strip. Martin took this photograph from the wall on the Princeton Avenue side of the Norfolk and Western Railway passenger station. (Courtesy of Vera Hambrick.)

DRUM AND BUGLE CORPS IS BACK. Ellis Leon Martin took this photograph of the Bluefield Drum and Bugle Corps in front of the First National Bank building marching east on Princeton Avenue. Note the small group of African American children viewing the parade. There were approximately 4,000 black residents of Bluefield in 1945. (Courtesy of Vera Hambrick.)

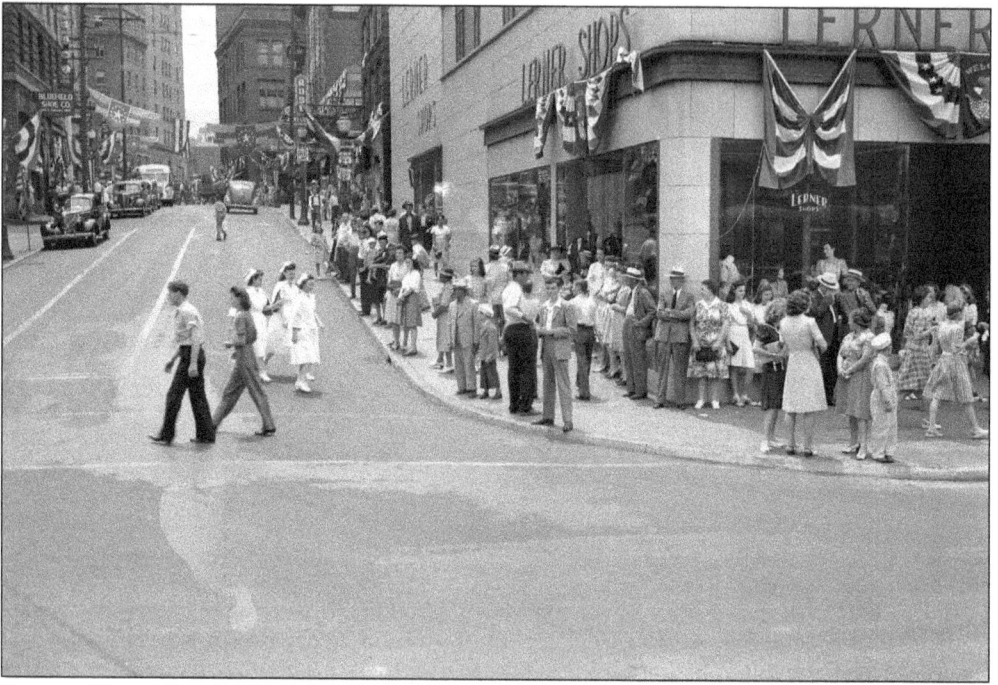

PARADE REST. People are shown here at the corner of Princeton Avenue and Federal Street gathering for the start of the July 4, 1945, Heroes' Day Parade. (Courtesy of Vera Hambrick.)

SACRIFICES. Mrs. Edward V. (Ocie) Devor of 137 Rollins Street in Bluefield, Virginia, rode the Army Mothers float as a five-star mother. She had three sons serving in the U.S. Navy and two in the U.S. Army. At the time of the parade, three of her sons were in the Pacific theater of the war, one was in New York, and another was in Texas. (Courtesy of Vera Hambrick.)

CLOSE ORDER DRILL. Members of the Bene Kedem Shrine Drill Team march on Princeton Avenue after passing Bland Street. Bluefield's Masonic temple was at 203 Federal Street at the time, across the street from the S. S. Kresge Store. The Shrine building housed the Masonic Trust Association as well as the Graham Ester Irene Dancing School. The drill team continues to perform at local parades, and Shriners continue to help crippled children and burn victims. (Courtesy of Vera Hambrick.)

CAR GO. The local Red Cross car saw plenty of action during the war, transporting messages from Bluefield to the U.S. Army Hospital in White Sulphur Springs and back as well as times when it was pressed into service for blackout preparedness drills. (Courtesy of Vera Hambrick.)

Floats on the Field. Mitchell Stadium—named for Emory P. Mitchell, Bluefield city manager in the 1930s and 1940s—was in its first decade when it served as the staging area for the Heroes' Day program following the parade. Mitchell was instrumental in bringing a Works Progress Administration camp to Bluefield, and WPA crews worked to build the field and other features of the two-state city park complex. Perhaps ironically, S.Sgt. J. I. "Junior" Spurrier, the man honored at the program, was a WPA worker before joining the army prior to passage of the Selective Training and Service Act of 1940. (Courtesy of Vera Hambrick.)

Paper Floats. Even the *Bluefield Daily Telegraph* and *Sunset News* had a float in the parade, but true to the newspaper's frugal reputation, the float broke down during the parade, according to the account of the event in the *Sunset News*. (Courtesy of Vera Hambrick.)

WHEREVER HE IS. The American Red Cross kept true to its motto, "Wherever he is," during the war. An unidentified Red Cross volunteer greeted parade attendees throughout the event. (Courtesy of Vera Hambrick.)

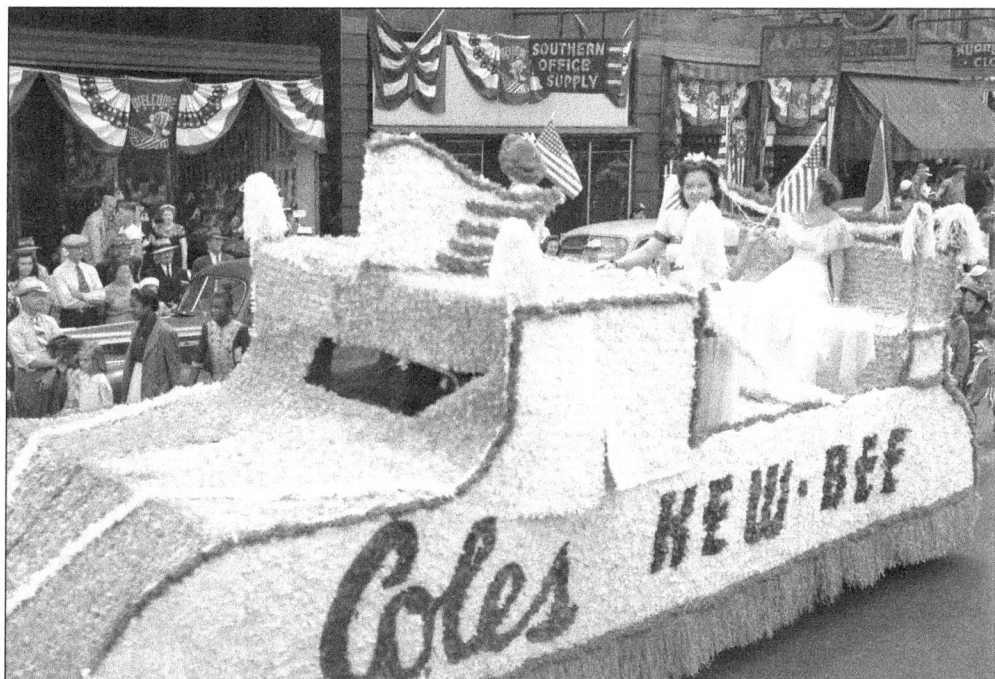

THREE FOR THE PARADE. Mary Ann Cole, Janet Cole, and Janet Welling rode the Cole Bakery float in the Heroes' Day Parade, according to an article in the *Sunset News*. The reporter wrote that the Cole float followed the Genoa High School Band in the order of the parade. (Courtesy of Vera Hambrick.)

BANK ON IT. Bluefield's stately First National Bank at the corner of Princeton Avenue and Federal Street serves as the backdrop of this July 4, 1945, photograph by Ellis Leon Martin. (Courtesy of Vera Hambrick.)

BUSES AND CARS. By 1945, most of the tracks that once carried Tri-City Traction streetcars around town had been recycled in the war effort, and Tri-City's bus fleet had become the prevalent public transportation around town. (Courtesy of Vera Hambrick.)

BAKERY PRIDE. A trio of young ladies who were not identified in the *Sunset News* account of the Heroes' Day Parade is shown riding the Feuchtenberger Bakeries float. The Feuchtenberger float followed the Salvation Army in the line of the parade. (Courtesy of Vera Hambrick.)

IN THE ARMY NOW. The high-ranking military personnel who participated in the Heroes' Day Parade arrived by train but were transported in military vehicles. (Courtesy of Vera Hambrick.)

CONGRESSMAN KEE. U.S. Representative John Kee (D., WV) of Bluefield delivers his remarks during the Heroes' Day program at Mitchell Stadium. "The home front is with them no matter where they go," Kee said of the heroes honored that day. (Courtesy of Vera Hambrick.)

SENATORIAL MESSAGE. U.S. Senator Chapman Revercomb (R., WV), a member of the military affairs committee of the U.S. Senate, had recently returned from a tour of the European theater of operations and provided an update of conditions there as part of his keynote speech. "The state honors and salutes you," Revercomb said to Staff Sergeant Spurrier. (Courtesy of Vera Hambrick.)

FOR THE HONOR OF THOSE IN SERVICE. Members of the Bluefield Service Men's Club represented the first civilian unit in the Heroes' Day Parade, following the Ashford General Hospital Band and parade dignitaries and immediately preceding the Army Mothers' float. The Bluefield Service Men's Club was organized in 1943 and disbanded soon after the end of the war. (Courtesy of Vera Hambrick.)

NATIONAL HERO. Lt. Col. Frank A. Hunter, commander of the prisoner of war camp in the Greenbrier Hotel in White Sulphur Springs, spoke of Staff Sergeant Spurrier as "a national hero," saying he served his nation "with high valor." Bluefield attorney George Richardson served as master of ceremonies for the event. (Courtesy of Vera Hambrick.)

TRIBUTE TO A HERO. Max Matz (center), chairman of the All-Community Committee, and Frank Archer (background, right), chairman of the finance committee, present a $5,000 U.S. savings bond to Staff Sergeant Spurrier (left) at the conclusion of the Heroes' Day program. (Courtesy of Vera Hambrick.)

Honoring Those Who Served. An unidentified soldier is shown carrying an American flag and riding a horse on Princeton Avenue during the Heroes' Day Parade. Although S.Sgt. J. I. "Junior" Spurrier was the guest of honor at the parade, the event was held to recognize the sacrifices of the men and women who served in World War II as well as to honor all of the people who sacrificed during the war. (Courtesy of Vera Hambrick.)

Where the Girls Are. Ellis Leon Martin couldn't resist taking another photograph of the American Legion float as it moved past his position on the parade route. (Courtesy of Vera Hambrick.)

WELCOME HOME. S.Sgt. J. I. "Junior" Spurrier was only 22 years of age when the City of Bluefield honored him during the program at Mitchell Stadium at the conclusion of the Heroes' Day Parade. About 30,000 people were in attendance. On the day before the event, a smiling Junior Spurrier registered for the draft, but at that point in his young life, he had already been awarded the nation's highest medal for valor, the Congressional Medal of Honor. Syd Barksdale of the *Sunset News* characterized Spurrier as "a likeable youth, a good example of the GI Joes who have won the European war and who are now victoriously fighting in the Pacific." Staff Sergeant Spurrier was awarded the Medal of Honor for his single-handed capture of the German-held town of Achain, France, on November 14, 1944. Although he was born in Coeburn, Virginia, his father, J. I. Spurrier, was living at 1632 Princeton Avenue in Bluefield, West Virginia, when his son entered the army. (Courtesy of Vera Hambrick.)

Four

UNDERSTANDING PEACE

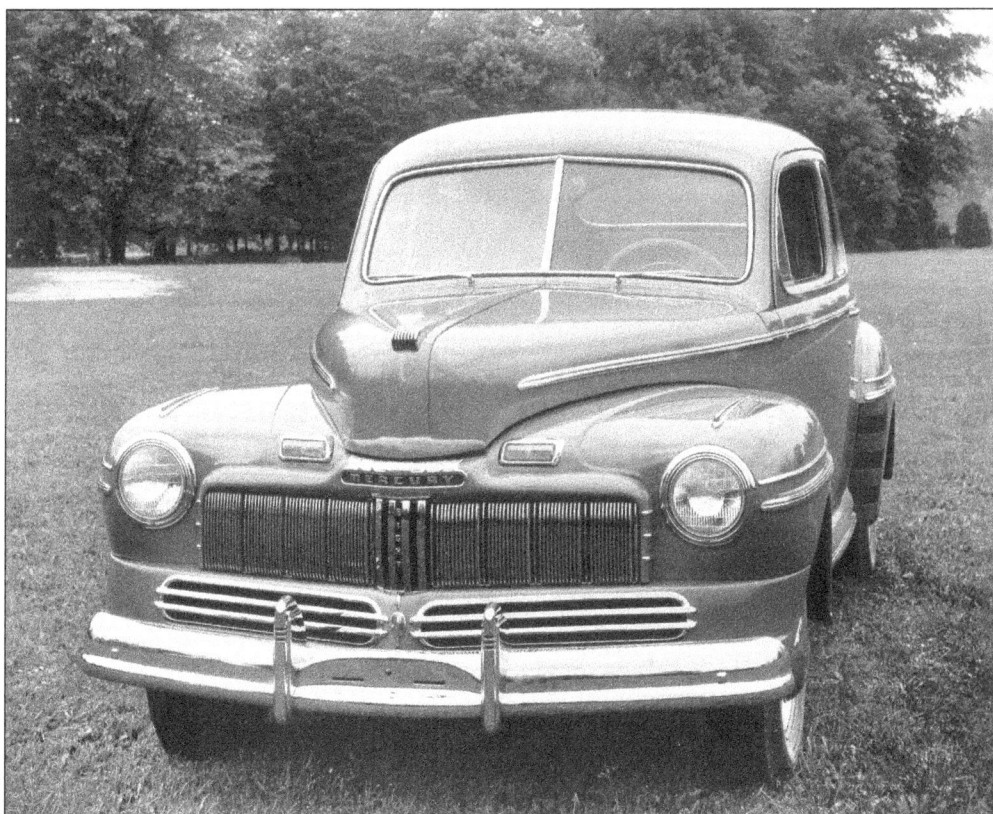

THE 1946 MODELS. After several years of committing resources to the war effort, American car manufacturers were able to use steel again and retooled factories to supply American consumers with automobiles. The 1946 Mercury sedan shown here was available at the Mercer Garage at 717 Raleigh Street. (Courtesy of Joe Davidson.)

A City Returns to Normal. An unidentified city worker fills a pothole on Bland Street with a shovelful of gravel under the watchful eyes of Sgt. Robert "Bobby" Jones of the Bluefield Police Department. Mel Grubb took the photograph near the intersection of Bland and Ramsey Streets, with the *Bluefield Daily Telegraph* building in the background and Cole Bakery's "Kew-Bee Bread" billboard on Stoney Ridge overlooking the city. Sergeant Jones and his wife, Kathryn T. Jones, lived at 1715 1/2 Bluefield Avenue. (Photograph by Mel Grubb.)

Can I Get an Amen? Bluefield's faith-based community has always been one of the city's strong points. Although this pastor is unidentified, the city had scores of worship centers representing African Methodist Episcopal, Apostolic, Baptist, Christian, Church of God, Episcopal, Hebrew, Holiness, Lutheran, Methodist, Mormon, Nazarene, Presbyterian, Roman Catholic, and more than a dozen other faiths. (Photograph by Mel Grubb.)

STEAM POWER. The later 1940s marked a major shift in the locomotive power that drove the mighty Norfolk and Western trains through the city of Bluefield. This photograph was taken during a test of steam power in the Bluefield yard in 1945. The picture served as the cover photograph on the author's first book in Arcadia Publishing's Images of America series, titled *Bluefield, West Virginia*, published in 2000. (Courtesy of the Eastern Regional Coal Archives.)

MAN POWER. While steam supplied the power for the engines that pulled the trains through Bluefield, people supplied the ingenuity to keep the trains on the track. An unidentified steam locomotive engineer operates a big Norfolk and Western locomotive. (Photograph by Mel Grubb.)

POWER OF CHANGE. These two locomotives were tested for power during the steam test of 1945. Bluefield was essentially a pasture in 1882, but the coming of the Northfork and Western Railway transformed the region into a city, primarily due to the natural gravity hump near where this photograph was taken. The hump or high point on the N&W mainline between the Ohio River and Atlantic shore enabled railroaders to assemble coal trains without using power. (Courtesy of the Eastern Regional Coal Archives.)

FOR HONOR AND COUNTRY. Members of Bluefield's Riley-Vest Post No. 9 of the American Legion are shown in 1947 presenting flags to be used along city streets during patriotic holidays. Mayor William C. Snyder, wearing a light-colored civilian hat, receives the flag, and Bluefield newsman H. Edward "Eddie" Steele wears a bow tie, second from the left in the front row. (From the author's collection.)

Graduation Day Parade Bluefield State Teacher[...]
May 31, 1938 Bluefield, W. Va.

DAWN OF A NEW ERA. Bluefield State College (BSC) celebrated its first half-century of providing an excellent education to African American students in 1945. Several graduates, like those in the class of 1938 shown here, went on to serve as officers and enlisted men during World War II. Their number included Atron (Rabbit) Hill, who was killed in action, as well as Capt. James T. Hubbard, Maj. Ralph Wilson, 1st Lt. William Toler, 1st Lt. William Green, and 1st Lt. John Flippin, among others. Many others, like Dr. William H. Gray Jr., former president of Florida A&M University; Dr. Lloyd E. Alexander of Fisk University; and Dr. Artis P. Graves of Morris Brown College went on to make an impact in the world of education. (Courtesy of BSC Archives.)

WORK OF ART. Noted West Virginia artist Joseph Dodd painted this Bluefield scene from his residence at 213 Park Street, where he lived during the time he served as director of the Bluefield State College art department. Dodd returned to BSC after his discharge from the army and died while walking home from the BSC campus on November 30, 1945. (Courtesy of Edwin D. Seymour.)

ART CLASS. Prof. W. E. "Eddie" Hebert is shown at the front of the classroom instructing Bluefield State College students on the finer points of fine arts in this photograph from the fall term of 1944, while Joseph Dodd was still in the service. Professor Hebert continued Dodd's legacy of excellence for decades after his colleague's untimely passing. Professor Hebert was also an excellent photographer. (Courtesy of Barbara Lewis.)

EMERGENCY LANDING. People attending a New Year's Eve party sponsored by the Clover Club and held at the Bluefield Country Club on December 31, 1945–January 1, 1946, were surprised when a huge twin-engine Conestoga aircraft owned by the Flying Tiger Lines crash-landed on the fairway of the third hole of the country club golf course at about 3:00 a.m. C. J. "Joe" Rosbert, pilot of the craft; copilot John Piney; and flight engineer O. E. Brown were uninjured in the crash. All four passengers—civilian W. E. Green; Henry R. Miller and John E. McGlaughlin, both of the U.S. Navy; and Lt. J. P. Bosco of the British Royal Navy—also escaped injury in the crash. Many Bluefielders heard the plane circling above the city searching for a landing place, and the WHIS radio announcer attempted to contact the plane. (Photograph by Mel Grubb.)

REPLACE ALL DIVOTS. The Flying Tigers Line airplane that crashed on the Bluefield Country Club golf course made the plane useless but did only minor damage to the No. 3 fairway, including knocking down an apple tree. The incident drew thousands of curiosity seekers to the crash site. The pilot, J. C. Rosbert, was a fighter pilot in the Pacific theater of World War II and also worked as one of the famous China National Aviation pilots who flew supplies from India to China over the Himalayan Mountains, known to pilots of the time as "the Hump." (Photograph by Mel Grubb.)

THE NEW MODELS ARE HERE. Alice Sue Richardson is looking good as she leans against the passenger door of a new 1946 Ford two-door convertible in the Mercer Garage showroom on Raleigh Street in Bluefield. Pete Barrow, Mercer Garage sales manager (to Richardson's right), and Jesse F. Willis, manager of the garage, are also pictured. Alice Sue Richardson was an office secretary at the Richardson and Kemper law firm. (Courtesy of Joe Davidson.)

HOME COOKING. Pearl Faulkner (right) is shown working with the unidentified wives of two coal miners, teaching them how to prepare food for the winter by canning fruits and vegetables as part of a program sponsored by the state school board. The program originated in 1944, and the facility in Bluefield, shown here, was one of 30 where coal miners' wives could learn how to preserve food by canning at a cost of 3¢ per jar. (Courtesy of the Eastern Regional Coal Archives.)

COME AND GET IT. An unidentified homemaker is shown with mixing bowl and utensils in hand, apparently ready to prepare a meal. (Photograph by Mel Grubb.)

ROAD SHOW. The gentlemen gathered here in the mid-1940s at the Bluefield Country Club were dedicated to opening up the region through good roads, including making U.S. Route 460 a four-lane highway and developing Interstate 77. The group includes, in no particular order, Ernest G. Otey, Jim Gills, H. Edward "Eddie" Steele, Hudson Huffard, and Don Martensen, all of Bluefield; Ned Turner of Glen Lyn, Virginia; Livingston Dillow of Pearisburg, Virginia; and two other unidentified gentlemen from Giles County, Virginia. (From the author's collection.)

CHAMPIONS OF EDUCATION. Members of the black business community as well as educators in the African American public schools are shown in a meeting in the Genoa High School. From left to right are two unidentified; Roscoe Chambers, a teacher at Genoa; A. A. Lawrence; unidentified; G. H. "Barney" Sinkford; two unidentified; Dr. Richard Brown, principal of Genoa High School; Elhanier Willis, coach of football and basketball at Genoa; and six unidentified. (Courtesy of Charles Thompson.)

NOBEL BOUND. Dr. John Forbes Nash Jr. graduated from Beaver High School in Bluefield in 1945, and within five years received an undergraduate and a master's degree from Carnegie Tech in Pittsburgh, Pennsylvania, as well as his doctorate from Princeton University, where his dissertation on zero-sum games earned him a one-third share of the Nobel Prize in Economics in 1994. (From the author's collection.)

THE ART OF MAN. The works of Joseph Eldridge Dodd, photographed here, have been on display in the Parkersburg Art Center and were included in John A. Cuthbert's book *Early Art and Artists of West Virginia*. Dodd studied his artistry and shared it with his students at Bluefield State College. (Courtesy of Edwin Seymour.)

ALL CLEAR HERE. A Norfolk and Western Railway train conductor is shown hanging from a freight boxcar and motioning the all-clear sign to a locomotive engineer. The N&W's Bluefield yard continues to be one of the busiest yards in the (now) Norfolk Southern Railway system. (Photograph by Mel Grubb.)

ON THE HOME FRONT. Charles W. Dickey, a Railway Express agent in Bluefield, monitors freight shipments as they move through the Norfolk and Western Bluefield yard. Because of its strategic position in the Pocahontas Coalfields, local lore contends that Bluefield was a primary target of the Axis powers in terms of disrupting America's war effort, although the city remained safe during the war. Charles and his wife, Blanche I. Dickey, lived at 1208 Augusta Street. (Photograph by Mel Grubb.)

CITY ON THE MOVE. This late-1940s image of Bluefield was taken during the construction of the Scott Street Parking Facility, which can be seen slightly to the right of center near the 12-story-tall West Virginian Hotel. The Norfolk and Western Railway roundhouse in the upper left center of the photograph would become obsolete in the mid- to late-1950s, when the railroad switched from steam to diesel locomotives. (Photograph by Mel Grubb.)

SOMEWHERE TO PARK. The shift from public transportation on streetcars and trains to personal automobiles created a parking nightmare in downtown Bluefield. The municipal government took a major step forward in the late 1940s to address this problem through the construction of the Scott Street Parking Facility. (Courtesy of the Eastern Regional Coal Archives.)

UPTOWN. Federal Street, the center of the Bluefield business district, was alive with activity at the mid-mark of the 20th century. On almost any given day, people ventured into the downtown area, but the weekends proved to be the best time for city merchants, as people from surrounding communities descended on the downtown to shop and socialize. (From the author's collection.)

BEGINNING OF AN ERA. Corrine B. Barrow, the wife of Pete Barrow (sales manager of the Mercer Garage on Raleigh Street), is shown preparing to open the passenger door of a 1946 Mercury in December 1945. This was one of the first new cars built after U.S. automakers shifted from war production back to making domestic products. Four of the six men behind Barrow include Jesse F. Willis, manager; Okie Garrett, parts manager; Harry Leist, shop foreman; and Hubert Winfrey. Harry Leist's son, Howard Leist, served as Bluefield city manager in the late 1960s. The four men near the Christmas tree are unidentified. (Courtesy of Joe Davidson.)

Five

BLUEFIELDERS ON THE JOB

HAPPY HATTER. Ethyl Calfee is shown surrounded by hats at Stella Jones's millinery shop at 623 Bland Street. Bluefielders were up to date with all the latest fashions in 1947. (Photograph by Mel Grubb.)

MODERN ERA LAMPLIGHTER. Garnett S. "Doc" Helton, a serviceman for Appalachian Power Company, had a unique occupation in the 1940s. Each business day at dusk, Helton went from store to store through the downtown business district, turning on the outdoor lighting at the store. When 11:00 p.m., rolled around, Helton went from store to store turning the exterior lights back off. Doc Helton and his wife, Bertie, lived on Cumberland Road. (Photograph by Mel Grubb.)

A SWITCH IN TIME. Garnett "Doc" Helton is shown stretching to reach the light switch on the exterior of Dr. J. I. "Jay" Rodgin's optometry shop at 306 Bland Street. (Photograph by Mel Grubb.)

SOMETHING TO BE TANK FULL FOR. Roba W. Smith is shown here topping off a gas tank at his station, R. W. Smith's Esso, at 1000 Princeton Avenue on the corner of Monroe Street. There was also a Smith's Esso station at 1000 Bluefield Avenue at Spruce Street. Roba Smith earned a reputation as an honest businessman who would let his customers, of all races, run a tab when times were hard and settle up when they could. (Photograph by Mel Grubb.)

NUMBER PLEASE. Mrs. Willie White supervises the switchboard operators at the Bluefield Telephone Company at 210 Bland Street. The company's slogan was "Nothing gives so much for so little," and Bluefield offered connections to exchanges in Bluefield, Bramwell, Davy, Keystone, Kimball, Northfork, Princeton, and Welch in West Virginia and to Bluefield, Grundy, Pocahontas, Richlands, and Tazewell in Virginia. White, the traffic supervisor at the phone company, lived at 620 Albemarle Street. (Photograph by Mel Grubb.)

ONE RINGY DINGY. An unidentified telephone information operator looks through the list of telephone numbers in the city to assist a caller with making a connection. (Photograph by Mel Grubb.)

BOTTLE TOP. Charles B. "Dutch" Cromer is shown inspecting bottles at the Coca-Cola bottling plant at 1217–1221 Bluefield Avenue. Cromer's family came from Dublin, Ireland, and he earned his nickname because his young friends thought he had a foreign accent. Charles Cromer Jr. (Dutch's son) served as city treasurer before his retirement around 2000. (Photograph by Mel Grubb.)

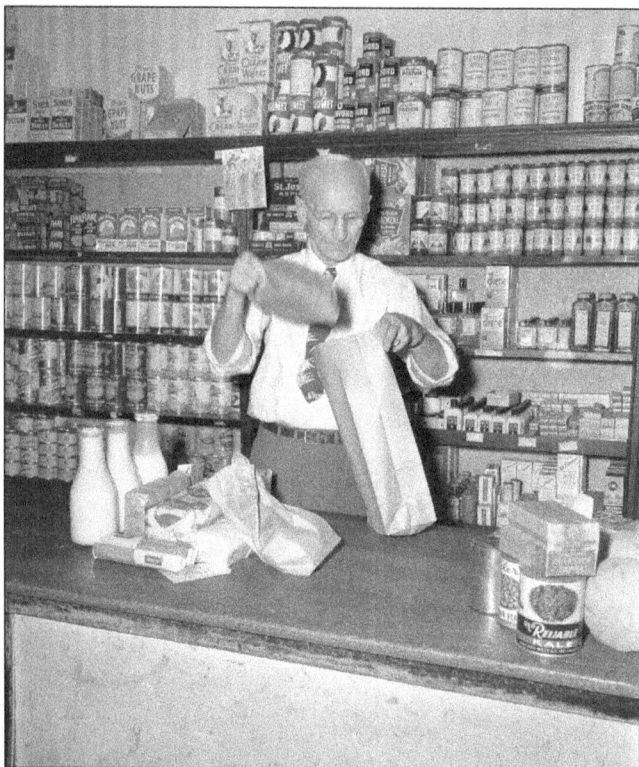

WE'VE GOT THAT. James K. "Jimmy" Porterfield of Porterfield's Grocery Store at 317 Bluefield Avenue was one of 58 grocery stores listed in the Bluefield City Directory in 1948. Porterfield and his wife, Margaret B. Porterfield, lived at 2926 Oak Grove Avenue. (Photograph by Mel Grubb.)

A REAL CLASSIC. By the end of the decade, the Classic Malt Shop had become a popular hangout for the bobby-socks crowd. The Classic was at 116 Federal Street, in the shop that previously housed Reed's Millinery. (Courtesy of Jack White.)

BANK SHOT. Russell A. Yarbrough, the trust officer of the First National Bank of Bluefield, is shown at his desk in the bank. Yarbrough and his wife, Edith, lived at 663 Shenandoah Avenue. (Photograph by Mel Grubb.)

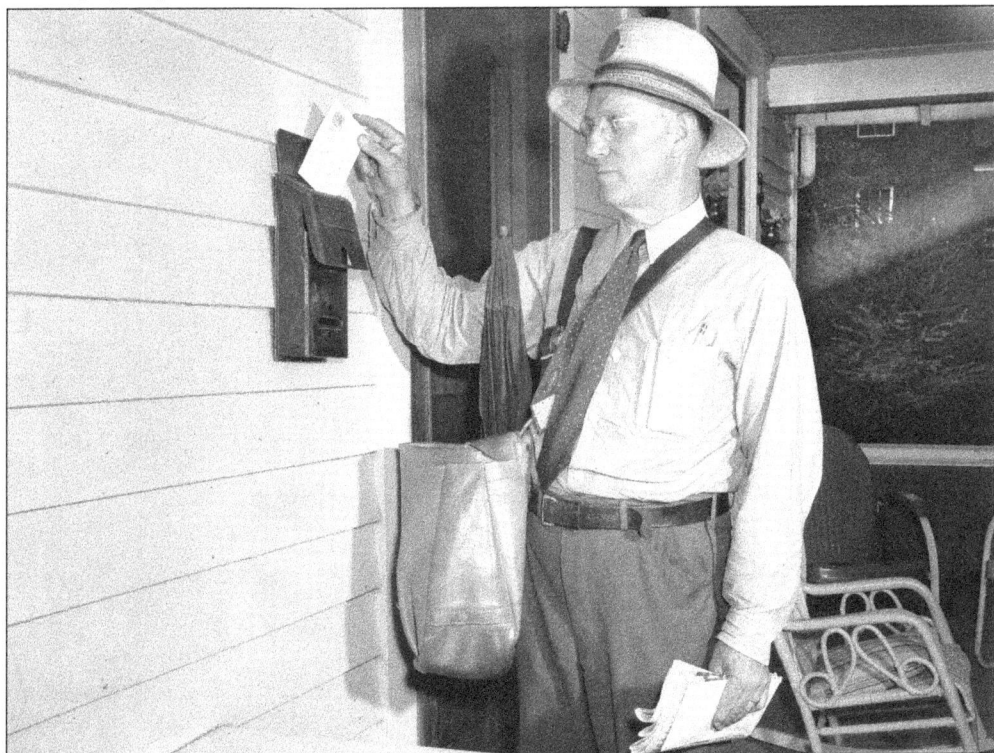

POSTMAN RINGS TWICE. Elijah S. Meadows, shown delivering the mail, had a reputation for being well informed. In the 1940s, mailmen in Bluefield delivered the mail twice daily. Meadows and his wife, Trixie, lived on Randolph Terrace. (Photograph by Mel Grubb.)

HOLD THE PHONE. Larry Dunn, a foreman at Appalachian Power Company, stays connected with his office via car phone. Dunn and his wife, Thelma, lived at 717 Albemarle Street. (Photograph by Mel Grubb.)

SNAIL MAIL. John R. French, then a clerk at the First National Bank of Bluefield, is shown handing letters to an unidentified bank employee. George Litz recalled that the young lady worked at the bank a short time before accepting a job as an airline stewardess. John and his wife, Lena French, lived at 2126 Reid Avenue. Lena French also worked at the bank and compiled the bank's history. (Photograph by Mel Grubb.)

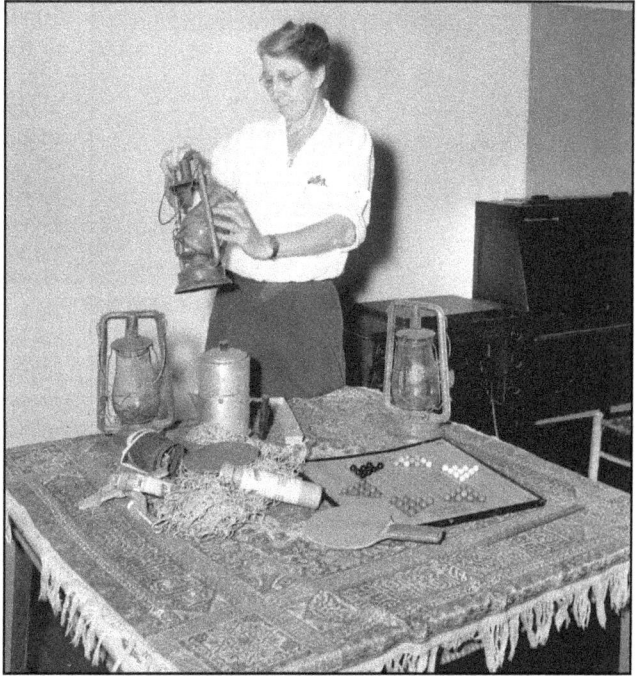

LIGHT WORK. Minnie E. "Min" Weaver was a tireless community servant who for many years was the general secretary of the Young Women's Christian Association (YWCA) when it was located at 515 1/2 Federal Street, in the same building that housed Wilson's Dry Goods and on the same side of the street as the Pinnacle Restaurant. Weaver is shown examining some antiques, probably for a sale to benefit the YWCA. (Photograph by Mel Grubb.)

CALLING ALL CARS. An unidentified police dispatcher is shown contacting an officer from the old dispatch office in the Bluefield City Hall that is now the Bluefield Area Arts Center at the corner of Bland and Ramsey Streets. The city police department was located where the Summit Theatre is now located. (Photograph by Mel Grubb.)

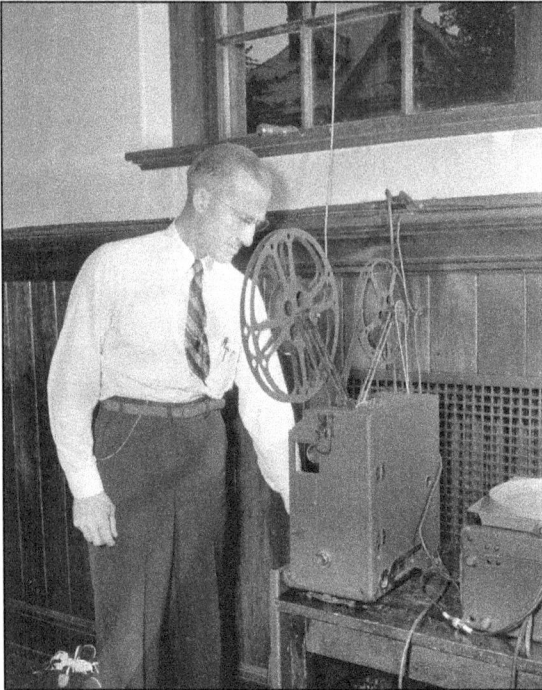

REEL TIME. Aubrey Stowers, principal at Ramsey School, is shown loading film in a 16-millimeter film projector at the school. Ramsey School was mentioned in one of Ripley's *Believe It or Not* books as being built on a hill so steep that it had seven different ground-level entrances. The famous American humorist Will Rogers once appeared on the Ramsey School auditorium stage and was quoted as saying that the thing he liked most about visiting Bluefield was that if he got tired while walking around town, he could just lean up against it. Stowers and his wife, Gladys, lived at 421 Union Street. (Photograph by Mel Grubb.)

DRAFTED. An unidentified draftsman works on what appears to be a drawing of the city business district. Alex Mahood was the city's leading architect in the 1940s, but other architects that served the area at that time included Lewis H. Nixon, whose office was also in the Law and Commerce Building, and Robert A. Sheffey, whose office was in the Appalachian Electric Power building at 606 Bland Street. (Photograph by Mel Grubb.)

BAND ON THE RUN. Richard Wellock, director of Bluefield's Beaver High School band, is shown striking a pose as if to lead the band in a selection. In 1947, Sydnor "Sid" Barksdale, editor of the *Sunset News*, the city's afternoon paper, asked Mel Grubb, who at that time was a clerk at Nelson's Photo Supply Company at 618 Federal Street and was a part-time stringer photographer for the newspaper, to go around the city and photograph the people of Bluefield. Mel Grubb's wife-to-be, June H. Deaumer, was the society editor of the *Bluefield Daily Telegraph*, the city's morning paper and Barksdale's philosophical opposite. The *Sunset News* had Democratic leanings, and the *Daily Telegraph*, under editor/publisher Hugh Ike Shott, gave staunch support to the Republican Party. The Shott family owned both newspapers, but each newspaper enjoyed political autonomy. (Photograph by Mel Grubb.)

LOOK AT THE BIRDIE. Helen Chandler is shown taking a portrait in the Breckenridge Studio on the second floor (room 212) of the First National Bank building on Princeton Avenue. Helen was the daughter of the studio founder, and she and her husband, Robert W. Chandler, continued the family's tradition of excellence in portrait photography. The Chandlers lived at 2312 Spring Garden Drive. (Photograph by Mel Grubb.)

SELF PORTRAIT. Mel Grubb is shown using the enlarger at Nelson's Photo Supply, where he worked as a clerk in 1947. When Sid Barksdale asked him to take the series of portraits of Bluefielders on the job, he knew a few of the people, like Helen Chandler, although most of them were names on an assignment sheet. Hugh Ike Shott served in the House of Representatives and completed an unexpired term in the U.S. Senate until Chapman Revercomb was elected in 1942. U.S. Senator Robert C. Byrd (D., WV) followed Revercomb in the office in 1958. After the Shott family folded the *Sunset News and Observer* in 1971, Barksdale went to work for Byrd as a speechwriter. (Self portrait by Mel Grubb.)

FURNITURE ARTISTRY. Morris W. Steiner is shown making a chair in his factory at 129 Roanoke Street in Bluefield. Although he did sell some of his products locally, Steiner's furniture was very popular among furniture buyers in Texas. Morris's brother, Leo Steiner, played football for the University of Tennessee and had the honor of playing in four consecutive bowl games for the Volunteers. Morris Steiner lived in the family home at 361 Union Street. (Photograph by Mel Grubb.)

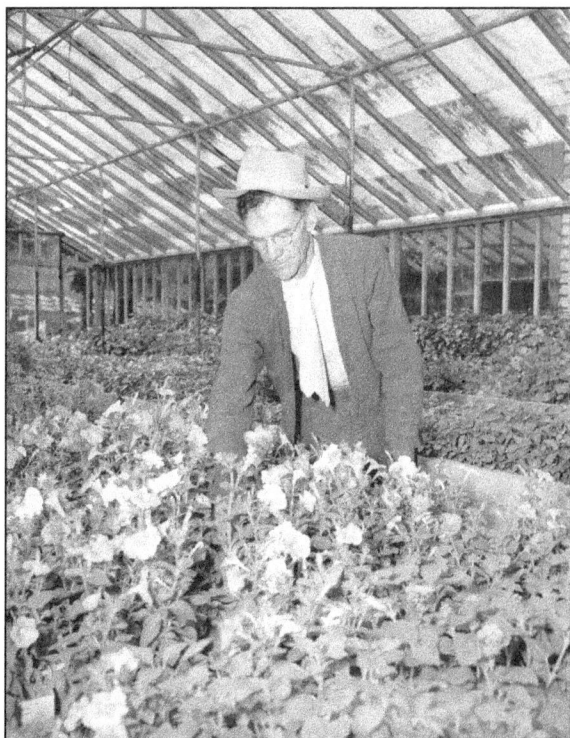

IN THE GARDEN. Donald N. Hume tends his petunias at his greenhouse at 706–708 Bluefield Avenue. Hume had been a serviceman for Bluefield Hardware before opening a greenhouse where he raised flowers and bedded tomato plants. Hume's wife, Anne, was a native of Rome, Georgia. (Photograph by Mel Grubb.)

POTTED PLANT. A florist examines a pot of chrysanthemums at Bluefield Floral Company at 520 Federal Street. The company advertised day and night delivery. (Photograph by Mel Grubb.)

UNIQUE EXPERIENCE. William S. "Bill" Hendricks is shown checking the tags for a customer at Unique Cleaners at 1231 Bland Street in Bluefield's Midtown Section. Hendricks and his wife, Margaret J. Hendricks, lived at 2021 Wythe Avenue. (Photograph by Mel Grubb.)

MONUMENTAL TASK. Mel Grubb ventured across the state line to photograph Cisle Ruble taking his work for granite at Bluefield Monument Company, located at 430 Virginia Avenue in Bluefield, Virginia. Ruble and his wife, Mattie, lived at Rural Delivery 1, Bluefield, Virginia. (Photograph by Mel Grubb.)

Six

DAWN OF A NEW ERA

TRUCKING. William Y. "Billy" Cooper, a member of the famous Cooper coal baron family from Bramwell, West Virginia, got a job in sales for Dixie Appliance Company, a subsidiary of Bluefield Supply Company, after he returned home from military service in World War II. Cooper and his wife, Emaline, lived at 1013 Longview Drive. Cooper was a top salesman for Dixie Appliance from 1945 to 1984, winning more than 57 sales awards. (Courtesy of Susan Cooper Snyder.)

THE CITY IN FULL BLOOM. By 1950, the city of Bluefield had become a real metropolis, with a population in 1948 estimated at 24,000 people. The city was larger than other West Virginia cities, including Beckley (at 17,498), Moundsville (at 16,000), and even Morgantown (at 20,576), at the time and was the heart of southern West Virginia's coal transportation system. The aerial artistry of Mel Grubb helped city residents gain a better sense of themselves at mid-century. (Photograph by Mel Grubb.)

COLLEGE ON COMMERCE STREET. T. B. Cain, president of West Virginia Business College, created an excellent educational environment at the school that was accredited by the National Association of Accredited Schools and was at 529 1/2 Commerce Street. The college had a rival school—McLain Business College, founded by Thomas E. McLain and located on the sixth floor of the Coal and Coke Building. (Courtesy of Dick Copeland.)

SEAT OF GOVERNMENT. An unidentified clerk appears to be researching legal files, possibly in the clerk's office of the Elizabeth Kee Federal Building. The court opened in the first decade of the 20th century, and E. L. Bowman, maternal grandfather of Gen. Norman Schwarzkopf, served as the first clerk of the court. The modern courthouse was built in 1911. Elizabeth Kee followed her husband, John, in the House of Representatives from West Virginia's Fifth Congressional District, and their son, Jim Kee, followed his mother in the same office. (Photograph by Mel Grubb.)

DOCUMENT SEARCH. Another unidentified clerk is looking through a file cabinet. Like many cities, Bluefield's progress generated a lot of paperwork. (Photograph by Mel Grubb.)

BUSINESS AS USUAL. World War II stimulated the coal industry in southern West Virginia, and Bluefield grew as the hub of the region's coal industry. In the early 1930s, the Bluefield-based Pocahontas Operators Association established the Southern Appalachian Industrial Exhibit, a forerunner of what is now known as the Bluefield Coal Show. The industrial exhibit was based in the Norfolk and Western Railway freight station on Bluefield Avenue and provided an opportunity for companies to display the state-of-the-art equipment of the modern coal industry, as shown in this photograph from the 1940s. (Courtesy of the Eastern Regional Coal Archives.)

CLEAN SWEEP. Janice Frazier, a student and the daughter of Charles and Bertha Frazier of College Avenue in Bluefield, is shown at a late-1940s Southern Appalachian Industrial Exhibit demonstrating the operations of a track sweeper, designed to keep debris off railroad tracks and thus help prevent derailments. The industrial exhibits provided coal operators and railroad companies alike the opportunity to examine innovations in the coal industry. (Courtesy of the Eastern Regional Coal Archives.)

OVER DRAWN. An unidentified woman is shown using a tracing table to prepare a copy of a document. Note the map of the Middle East hanging in the background. Thanks to the diversity of Bluefield's population, the city has enjoyed a long tradition of relationships with other parts of the world. (Photograph by Mel Grubb.)

LOUNGE CAR SEATING. The Norfolk and Western Railway went to great lengths to introduce comfortable passenger cars on its new Powhatan Arrow passenger train service (Trains 25 and 26) between Norfolk, Virginia, and Cincinnati, Ohio. The models shown here posed for a photo session prior to the launch of the new service. (Courtesy of Carlton Viar.)

TRAVEL IN STYLE. The Powhatan Arrow was Norfolk and Western Railway's deluxe daytime passenger service, and the nighttime run of the same passenger train route between Norfolk, Virginia, and Cincinnati, Ohio, was known as the Princess Pocahontas, the first train named after a woman. The N&W launched the Powhatan Arrow on April 28, 1946. (Courtesy of Carlton Viar.)

STREAMLINED POWER. The Norfolk and Western streamlined J-Class locomotives supplied the pull for the Powhatan Arrow, Princess Pocahontas, and other stylish passenger trains. The N&W built a total of 13 of the streamlined J-Class 600 Series locomotives at the railroad's shops in Roanoke, Virginia, including the first two, the 600 and 601, shown here. (Courtesy of Elizabeth Devault Gearheart and the Graham Historical Society.)

FACULTY MATTERS. The faculty of Bluefield State College, with BSC president Dr. Henry Lake Dickason in the center foreground (front row, fourth from the left), posed for this photograph that was part of the college's "Semi-Centennial Bulletin." The state legislature passed a law on March 5, 1943, formally changing the name of the college from Bluefield State Teachers' College to Bluefield State College. Dr. Dickason promised "larger and broader services" for BSC in "the post-war era." (Courtesy of Barbara Lewis.)

TEAM SPORT. The Genoa High School 1948–1949 team scorched the local hardwood courts. From left to right are (first row) Monroe Crouther, Earl Clayton, Cecil Harmon, Charles Brogdon, Vandy Miller, and coach Elhanier Willis; (second row) Clarence Wade (manager), James Francisco, Willie Hurt, William Small, William Tynes, Edward Anthony, and Isaiah Wright. (Courtesy of Charles Thompson.)

TOUGH YEAR. The Genoa High School Wildcats had a tough 1948 season, posting a 3-5-1 record. From left to right are (first row) Robert Morgan, James Witten, Leon Joiner, Cecil Harmon, Lloyd Brown, Francis Gray, and Charles Brogden; (second row) Monroe Crouthers, Gilbert Stone, Clarence Wade, Samuel Hairston, Robert Crews, Vandy Miller, Marion Salley, and Earl Clayton; (third row) Edward Randolph, Bernard Bowling, William Tynes, Joe Hairston, Richard Marshall, Bruce Steele and James Francisco; (fourth row) Edward Anthony, Robert T. English, Earl Stone, and coach Elhanier Willis. (Courtesy of Charles Thompson.)

ALL GROWN UP. This city street scene from around 1950 shows Federal Street and the heart of downtown Bluefield all grown up with somewhere to go. During the late 1940s and well into the 1950s, the streets of downtown Bluefield were jammed with people all year round, shopping, visiting friends, or visiting the local restaurants. (Courtesy of *Bluefield Daily Telegraph* archives.)

SOUND SENSATION. The Beaver High School a cappella choir, under the direction of Elizabeth R. Shelton, was one of the best-known performance ensembles in the region. All Beaver students were required to take a vocal music class, but only the best singers in the school were invited to participate in the a cappella choir. Shelton lived near the school at 108 Rogers Street. (Courtesy of the Eastern Regional Coal Archives.)

TICKER TAPE PARADE.
Benjamin A. BeCraft was
the manager of the Bluefield
Western Union office at 311
Federal Street in the Law
and Commerce Building.
Western Union kept several
young boys in the city busy by
having them deliver messages
throughout the city. BeCraft
and his wife, Faye, lived at 1310
Roy Avenue. (Photograph by
Mel Grubb.)

WIRED COMMUNICATIONS.
An unidentified technician is
shown troubleshooting some
of the wiring of the complex
Strother Switch system,
which would provide an
automated switching process
and dramatically reduce the
need for many telephone
switchboard operators.
(Photograph by Mel Grubb.)

PATTY CAKE, PATTY CAKE, BAKER'S MAN. An unidentified employee of Cole Baking Company, at the corner of Grant and Hardy Streets, is shown tending loaves of bread entering the wrapping machine. In addition to Cole's, the city was home to L. D. Feuchtenberger Bakeries, Inc., Frank's Bakery, National Biscuit Company, Sanitary Bakery, and Southern Baking Corporation. (Photograph by Mel Grubb.)

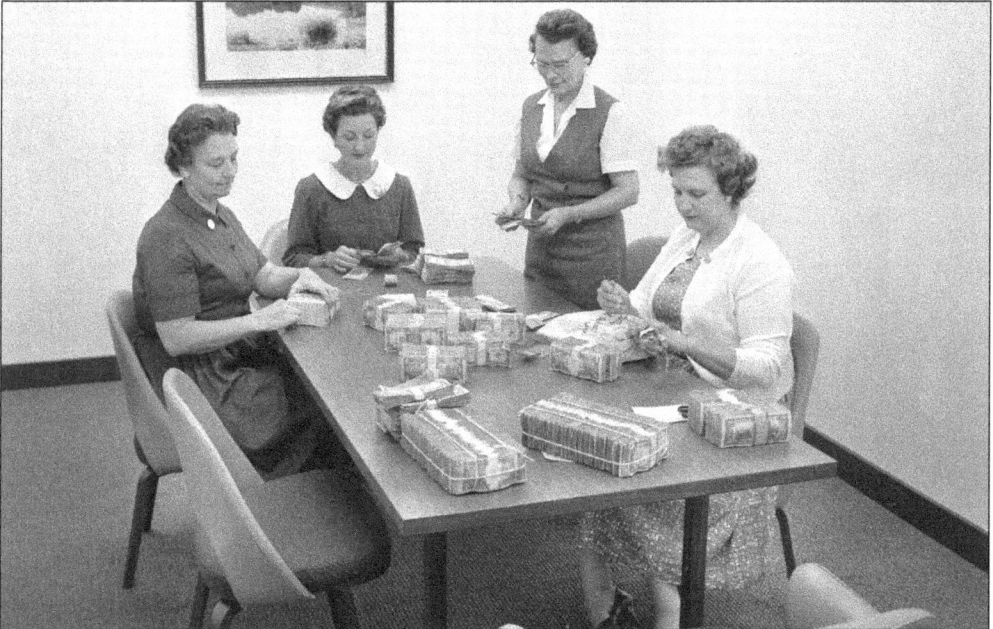

REAL BREAD. A group of First National Bank of Bluefield employees is shown counting cash, likely for distribution to local coal mines. From left to right are Ruth Kersey, Grace Sprinkle, a Mrs. McInturff, and Juanita Marrs. (Photograph by Mel Grubb.)

TICKET AGENT. This man was known to some in the area as "Russell," although his full name was not immediately recalled by those who helped identify the people in this book. He served as ticket agent for the Norfolk and Western Railway in Bluefield. (Photograph by Mel Grubb.)

CAN CAN. Wade H. Harry, of W. H. Harry and Company at 222 Princeton Avenue, examines cans of paint on his shelves. Harry and his wife, Nannie, lived at 123 Walnut Street. (Photograph by Mel Grubb.)

LOVE THAT MUDDY WATER. Art Riley recognized this man as Buck McCumber of the Sanitary Board of Bluefield. McCumber is shown working at the system's sewage treatment facility on Grassy Branch Road. The city would eventually install a larger treatment plant on the Ada Road and later still would work with the Town of Bluefield, Virginia, on the two-state Westside Sewage Treatment Plant located in Bluefield, Virginia. (Photograph by Mel Grubb.)

VALVE REPLACEMENT. An unidentified worker is shown working with a valve at the city's water treatment plant on the Ada Road outside the city limits. (Photograph by Mel Grubb.)

A SWITCH IN TIME SAVES NINE. This unidentified Norfolk and Western Railway worker is working in the East Yard tower of the busy Bluefield yard, throwing switches to regulate the flow of train traffic in that section. The Bluefield yard features the (now) Norfolk Southern Railway's two mainline tracks in and out of the city but expands to eight sets of tracks at the yard's widest point. (Photograph by Mel Grubb.)

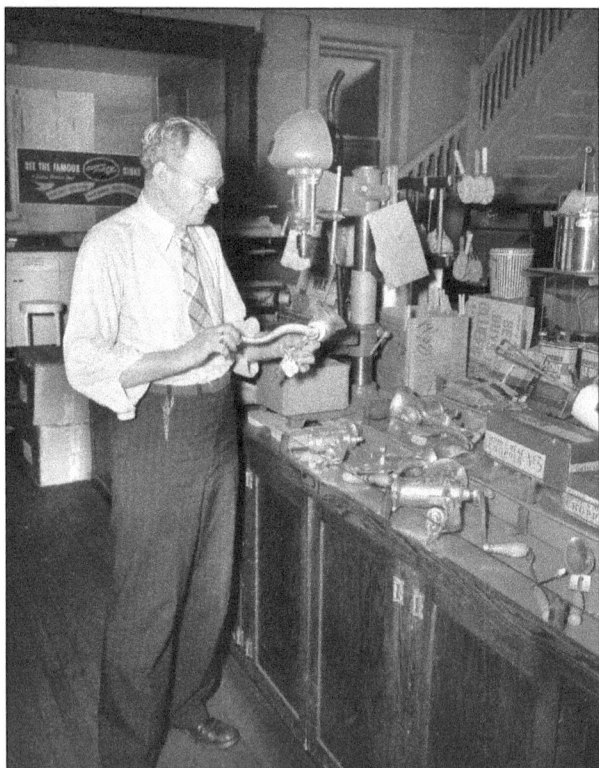

HAMBURGER MAN. An unidentified man turns the handle on a meat grinder. Meat grinders were an important part of almost every household before supermarkets started offering a variety of ground meats on a routine basis. (Photograph by Mel Grubb.)

HAPPY MEAL. John Dellis is shown at the cash register of the Liberty Café at 206 Bland Street with Lenius Harris in the background. Harris taught at Jones Street School and supplemented his earnings working as a waiter at several area restaurants as well as at the Bluefield Country Club. (Photograph by Melvin Grubb.)

LIKE A BRICK HOUSE. An unidentified bricklayer applies mortar with a trowel as he prepares to set another course of bricks in a wall. Masonry walls are on almost every street throughout Bluefield. (Photograph by Mel Grubb.)

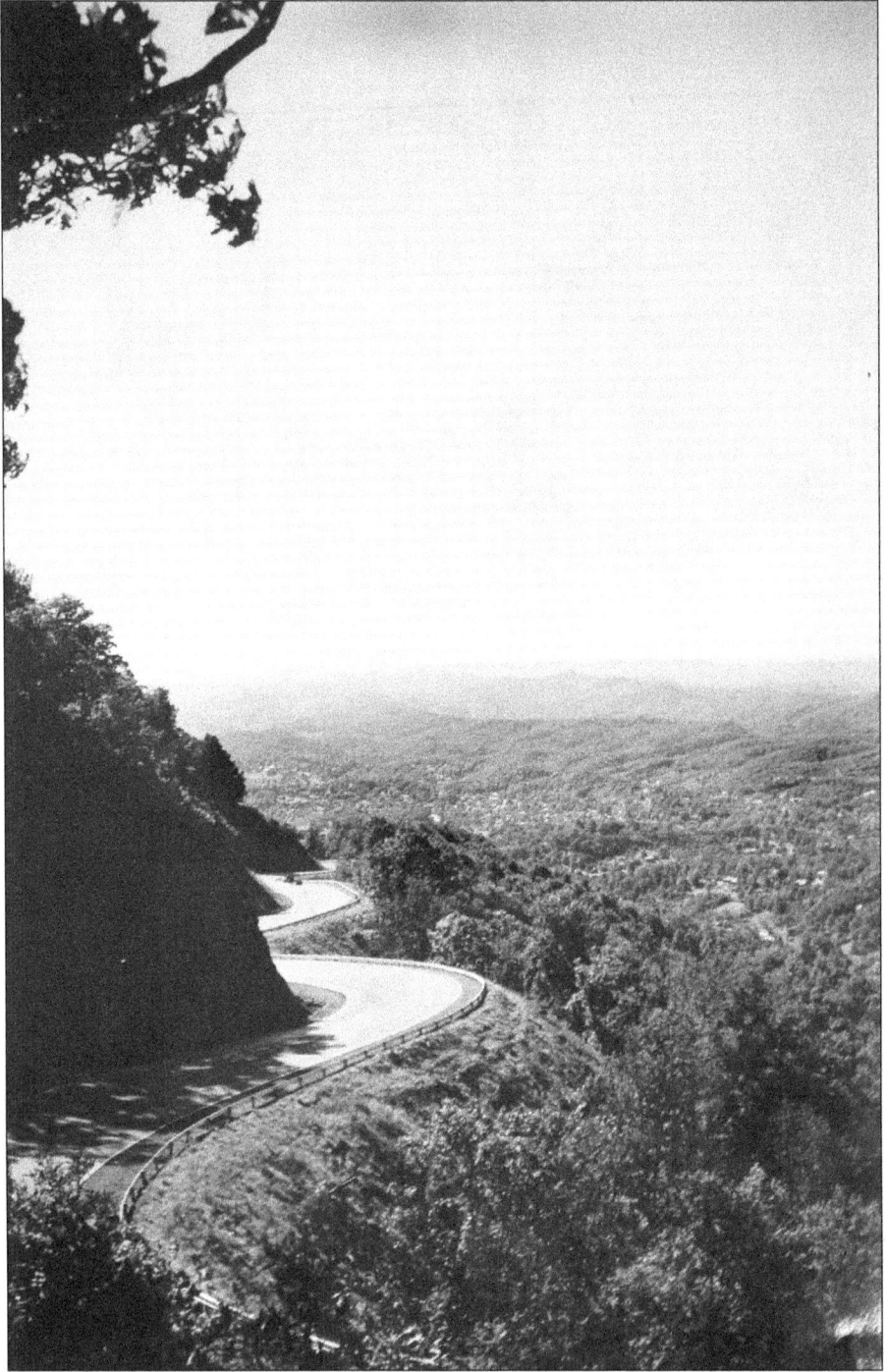

SCENIC BEAUTY. The East River Mountain Overlook provides a spectacular view of the city of Bluefield and the Allegheny mountain range that surrounds the city. By the end of the 1940s, civic leaders were already working to capitalize on the region's natural beauty and were laying the groundwork for developing a tourist stop at the top of the mountain. Those improvements would be realized in the 1950s. (Courtesy of the Eastern Regional Coal Archives.)

JOHN L. United Mine Workers of America president John L. Lewis is shown speaking during the union's meeting with the Bituminous Coal Operators' Association (BCOA) on May 25, 1949. Although Lewis was a frequent visitor to the region, this was his only public appearance in Bluefield. Laurence E. Tierney Jr. was president of the BCOA in the 1949 contract year. Tierney and his wife, Katharine Baker Tierney, lived at 625 Mountain View Avenue. Tierney was president of Flat Top National Bank, Citizens Underwriters Agency, Tierney Mining Company, and Laurence E. Tierney Land Company. (Photograph by Mel Grubb.)

BANK ON IT. Bluefield's First National Bank, shown here, was at the corner of Princeton Avenue and Federal Street. The city's other banks included the Flat Top National Bank at the corner of Federal and Raleigh Streets and the Commercial Bank of Bluefield, also on Federal Street on the corner of Commerce Street. (Photograph by Mel Grubb.)

INVINCIBLE. The 1942–1943 West Virginia Business College went through the women's basketball season undefeated. From left to right are Dorrell Martin, Anna Belle Catron, Sarah Gardner, Kathleen Breeding, Josephine Grisso, Oma Merritt, Delphia Gray, Frances Henderson, Regina Busko, Betty Thomas, Garnet Eatherly, and Helen Jean O'Neal. Coach Earl C. Gibson is not pictured. (Courtesy of Dick Copeland.)

120

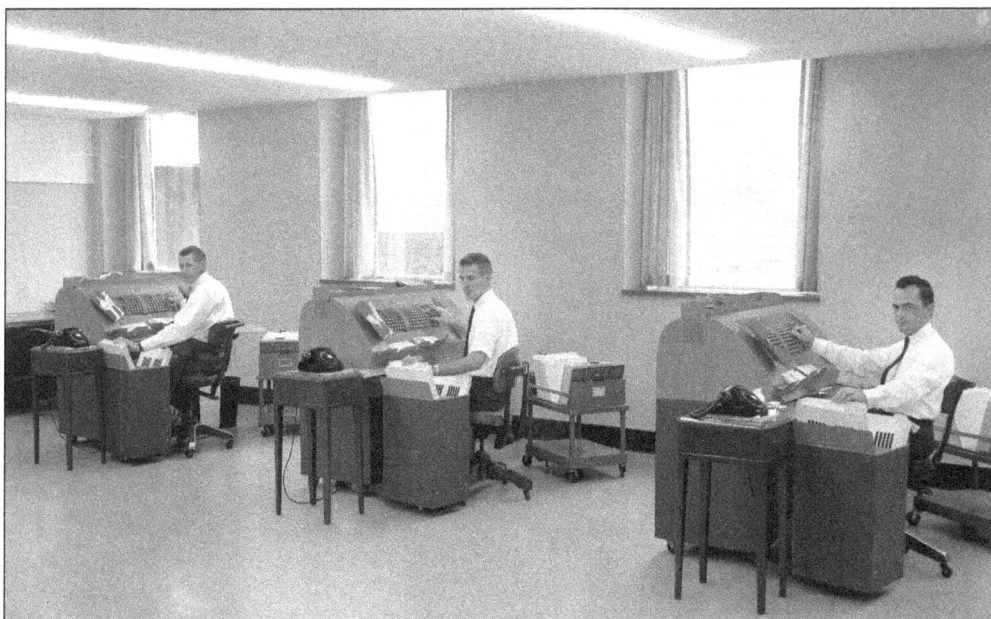

BANK JOB. These three men are working on ledger status posting in the bookkeeping department of the First National Bank of Bluefield. From left to right are Jack Cummings, Bill Belcher, and Bob Short. (Photograph by Mel Grubb.)

PAIR OF PANTS. Samuel Fine (right) was the manager of Bond's Two Pants Suit House at 336 Princeton Avenue. Fine and his wife, Nellie, lived at 912 College Avenue. James Harris (left) worked at Bond's and was a son of Milton and Dorothy Harris of Pearis Street in Bluefield. (Courtesy of Tom and Mary Jane Farmer.)

ONE FOR THE BOOKS. Dean Claude Willard Owen, professor of education and social science at Bluefield College (BC), reads a book in his office on the BC campus. Dean Owen lived on campus in House 5, College Row, and helped young people of the area in their pursuit of higher education. (Photograph by Mel Grubb.)

INSIDE STUFF. A Ford Motor Company technician examines the block of a V-8 motor. Harry Leist was the service manager of the Mercer Garage in 1947. Although all of the city's automobile dealerships had interesting asides, when customers brought their vehicles to the Mercer Garage for servicing, technicians took the vehicles to the top floor of the building on an elevator. The building now houses Warlick Furniture. (Photograph by Mel Grubb.)

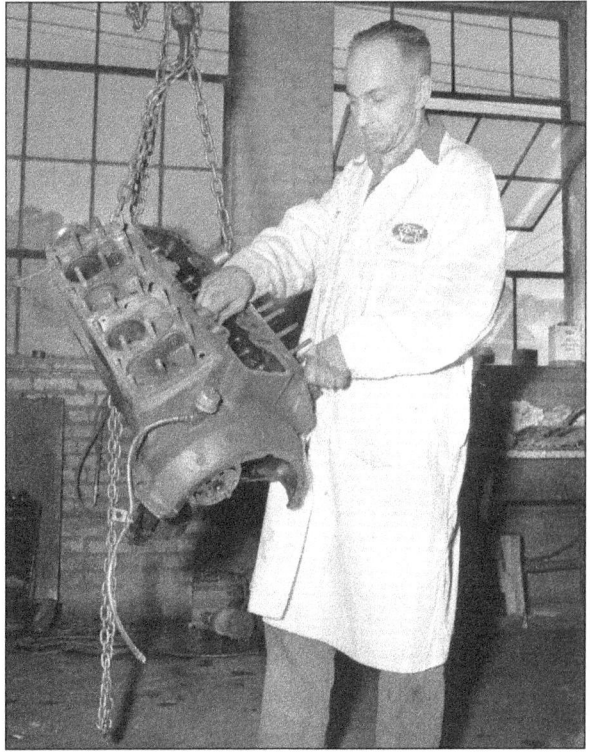

IT ALL ADDS UP. An unidentified clerk examines paperwork in the Norfolk and Western Railway offices on Princeton Avenue. Note the collectible Coca-Cola thermometer on the wall behind her. (Photograph by Mel Grubb.)

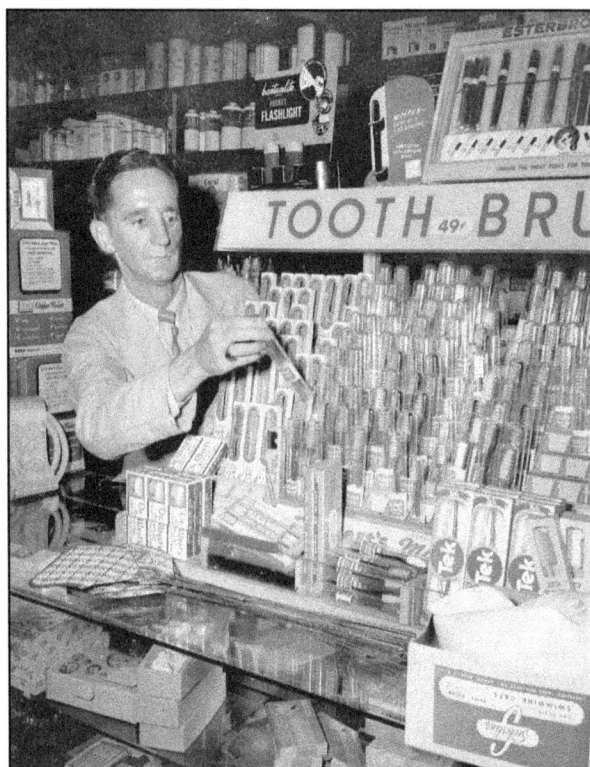

BRUSH UP. Edwin A. "Bus" McNeer, one of the great Beaver High School football players of his era, stocks the shelves with toothbrushes at the New Graham Pharmacy at 566 Virginia Street in Bluefield, Virginia. McNeer was the president/treasurer of New Graham Pharmacy in 1947. McNeer and his wife, Anne, lived at 505 Tazewell Avenue. (Photograph by Mel Grubb.)

HEALING ELIXIRS. Edwin A. "Bus" McNeer examines medicines on the shelf of New Graham Pharmacy in Bluefield, Virginia. New Graham continues to serve customers into the 21st century. (Photograph by Mel Grubb.)

OPEN WIDE. Dr. John S. Compton is shown examining his dental equipment at his office at 520 1/2 Princeton Avenue on the second floor of the First National Bank of Bluefield building. Dr. Compton lived at 101 Williams Street. (Photograph by Mel Grubb.)

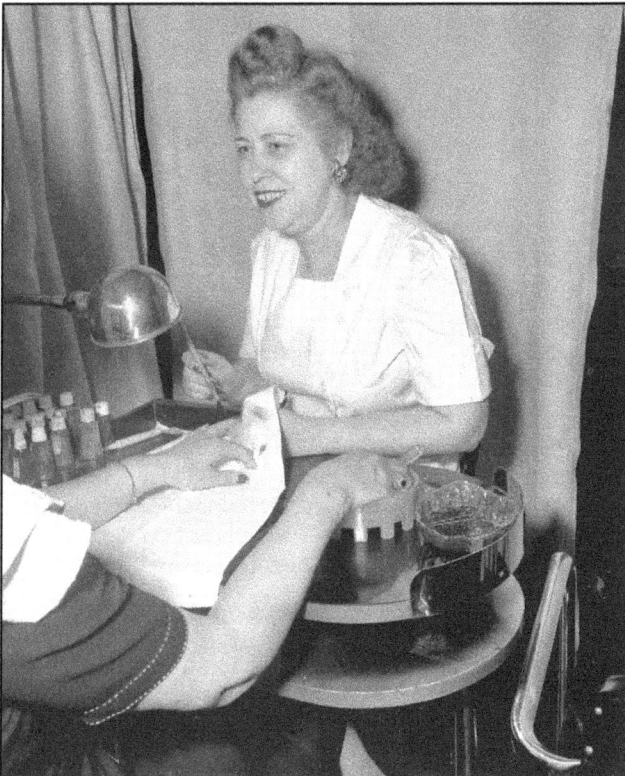

YOU'RE SOAKING IN IT. An unidentified manicurist applies polish on the fingernails of a customer. Bluefield had 19 beauty shops in 1947 as well as 14 barbershops. Many beauticians learned their trade at the Little French Beauty School on the eighth floor of the Coal and Coke Building. (Photograph by Mel Grubb.)

OPENING A NEW ERA. Norfolk and Western Railway officials marked the 1950 opening of the Elkhorn Tunnel on the mainline into McDowell County, West Virginia, by having a J-Class steam locomotive break through a tape at the tunnel entrance. The J-603 shown here later derailed near Tip Top, Virginia, and was scrapped. (Courtesy of the Eastern Regional Coal Archives.)

IN TUNE. Mattie Carroll examines one of her many miniature toy pianos, just one of the few things the young Bluefielder collected. Mattie was the daughter of Daniel M. and Lettie C. Carroll of 229 Union Street in Bluefield. Daniel Carroll opened Burkhart and Carroll Grocery Store in 1916. The store was at 1158 Bland Street and served the community until Daniel's youngest son, Arthur Carroll, closed it in 1978. Arthur's older brothers were both missionaries with the Southern Baptist Mission Board, with Daniel Carroll Jr. serving in Argentina and Webster Carroll serving in East Africa, with more than 30 years of service in Uganda. The Burkhart and Carroll Grocery Store was a missionary endeavor as well, serving the citizens of Bluefield through the years. (Photograph by Mel Grubb.)

Visit us at
arcadiapublishing.com

....

www.ingramcontent.com/pod-product-compliance
Lightning Source LLC
Chambersburg PA
CBHW080600110426
42813CB00006B/1359